Rosemary
SHRAGER'S
COOKERY COURSE

BBC Books, an imprint of Ebury Publishing
20 Vauxhall Bridge Road,
London SW1V 2SA

BBC Books is part of the Penguin Random House
group of companies whose addresses can be
found at global.penguinrandomhouse.com

Penguin
Random House
UK

First published by BBC Books in 2018
This edition published by BBC Books in 2021

www.penguin.co.uk

A CIP catalogue record for this book is
available from the British Library

ISBN 9781785947575

Publishing Director: Lizzy Gray
Editor: Charlotte Macdonald
Editor: Isabel Hayman-Brown
Project Editor: Jinny Johnson
Food Stylist: Lisa Harrison
Prop Stylist: Olivia Wardle
Design: Gemma Wilson
Production: Rebecca Jones

Colour origination by Altaimage, London
Printed and bound in Great Britain by Bell & Bain Ltd.,

The authorised representative in the EEA is
Penguin Random House Ireland, Morrison
Chambers, 32 Nassau Street, Dublin DO2 YH68

Penguin Random House is committed to a
sustainable future for our business, our readers
and our planet. This book is made from Forest
Stewardship Council® certified paper.

🥄 COOK'S NOTES 🥄

All spoon measures are level unless otherwise stated. One teaspoon is approximately 5ml and a tablespoon is about 15ml.

All eggs are large unless otherwise stated.

Use unsalted butter in recipes unless otherwise stated.

In some recipes I have said to seed chillies, otherwise I leave them in. It's up to you: if you want to reduce the heat, seed your chillies.

For zesting, use unwaxed fruit if possible. If you can't find unwaxed fruit, wash it well before zesting. I wash all fruit well anyway.

In a few recipes I specify curly or flatleaf parsley, but generally feel free to use whatever you prefer.

AUTHOR BIOGRAPHY

Rosemary Shrager is a cooking and food enthusiast. Her professional career includes periods working for Pierre Koffmann and Jean-Christophe Novelli, before running her own cookery courses at Amhuinnsuidhe Castle and Swinton Park. She now runs an eponymous cookery school in Tunbridge Wells, and appears regularly on television shows, such as The Real Marigold Hotel.

Rosemary SHRAGER'S

COOKERY COURSE

150 tried & tested recipes to be a better cook

BOOKS

CONTENTS

COOKING IS MY PASSION AND I HAVE LOVED IT ALL MY LIFE.
I come from a foodie family – my grandmother was an excellent cook and my grandfather adored good food. My family had a kitchen garden, our own rabbits and chickens, and cooking was such an important part of our lives. Cooking is in my blood.

I started my adult cooking life preparing directors' lunches in London and I was eager to learn everything I could. I didn't go to catering college – I taught myself. I devoured cookbooks, I asked questions, I watched other people. If I wanted to learn about meat, I went to a butchers' shop and begged them to show me how to bone and tie joints and how to get the best from different cuts. To learn about fish, I went to the fish markets and got them to teach me how to fillet. I would even ring chefs at the big hotels and ask them questions! In a way, I put myself through an apprenticeship and I kept books of notes and drawings, some of which I still have to this day.

I have met and learned from many wonderful people along the way, but perhaps my greatest mentor has been Pierre Koffmann, who is the most superb and inspirational chef and has taught me so much. He has encouraged me through all my various ventures.

My aim when writing this book wasn't just to make yet another cookery book. I want to inspire you, too and give you the confidence to experiment and challenge yourself. My philosophy is always to be inquisitive and bold, unafraid to try new things and new ideas – while not forgetting the importance of knowing the basic techniques. So that is why in this book I have included recipes for boiled eggs, green salad and plain rice as well as soufflés, pies and even a four-bird roast! If you have the basics right, your cooking is more likely to be successful. Each chapter starts with very simple recipes and takes you through to more challenging dishes.

The important thing is to know how to get the best from your ingredients and how to add flavour. For instance, if you have a bundle of perfect new season's English asparagus, serve it as simply as possible, with nothing more than butter and plenty of seasoning. But if you have a bag of spring greens you might like to bring them to life by adding flavours such as garlic, juniper, bacon or whatever you like.

'Each chapter starts with very simple recipes and takes you through to more challenging dishes.'

I want to encourage people not only to cook but also to enjoy cooking. It doesn't have to be a chore. Yes, it's hard when you have a family and you need to produce meals day in and day out, but try some different dishes once in a while and add to your repertoire. It'll make it more fun for you as well as the family.

MY COOKERY SCHOOL

Because I love cooking and have always been fascinated by food, I wanted to share my passion with other people. I learned the hard way – on the hoof, as it were – but I wanted to help others gain knowledge more easily.

I'm in partnership with the Hadlow Group, which has a number of colleges including West Kent and Ashford, and we have a cookery school at Tunbridge Wells. There we run our Rosemary Shrager apprenticeships as well as a range of cookery courses for anyone who wants to learn to cook.

My aim in all my teaching is to inspire my students and share my own passion for food.

When teaching beginners, I like to feel I send people away with a greater knowledge of techniques and the confidence to use them to enjoy and experiment with their cooking. I hope for the same with this book.

'Because I love cooking and have always been fascinated by food, I wanted to share my passion with other people.'

GOLDEN RULES

I'm all for breaking rules but there are some kitchen habits I like to stick to.

- Buy everything as fresh as possible. Seek out good producers for your ingredients – supermarkets have their place, but look at local farms and markets as well to get the best.
- Be organised when preparing food. Keep your ingredients on your left and prepped food on your right.
- When preparing ingredients, complete one task before starting the next. For example, skin all your tomatoes, then chop them all – don't peel one, then chop it, then go back to peeling. It's just not efficient.
- Clear up as you go along. Mess is stressful.
- Make sure you have good chopping boards and use separate ones for meat, poultry, fish and vegetables. You can get boards in different colours, which is helpful for keeping track of things.
- Try to build flavour in your dishes and always season carefully.
- Don't be afraid to think outside the box. If a recipe is for chicken but it is the game season, try using a pheasant instead.

ADDING FLAVOUR

Many prepared foods contained large amounts of salt and this is what can do us harm, not the salt you add to the food you cook – as long as you don't overdo it. I use fine sea salt or flaked sea salt according to the needs of the recipe.

Pepper is a spice and you don't need to use it in everything. I do love the flavour of black pepper but I don't always like to see the little black flecks on my food, so I sometimes prefer white pepper.

BUTTER

I like French butter for cooking as it is purer and contains fewer milk solids, so doesn't burn as easily. I prefer to use unsalted butter as I can then add my own seasoning. When sautéing with butter, I use a little oil as well – otherwise the butter tends to burn quickly.

Generally I use unsalted butter for cooking, but I do adore good strong salted butter on my toast for breakfast – one of my favourite eating moments!

PAIRING HERBS

One way of building flavour in your cooking is by the clever use of herbs. The following lists some suggestions for herb pairings. Remember that if you are using dried herbs, you need only about a third of the amount of fresh as the flavour of dried is more intense.

Basil
Tomatoes, vegetables, salad, pasta, chicken lamb, pork.

Coriander
Tomatoes, vegetables, beans, chicken.

Mint
Sauces, coulis, sweet dishes, beans, chicken, pork, lamb.

Sage
Vegetables, pasta, gnocchi, stuffings, pork sausages, beef.

Bay leaves
Soups, pasta sauces, fish, casseroles with beef, lamb or pork.

Dill
Eggs, vegetables, fish, shellfish, chicken, pork.

Oregano
Soups, tomatoes, beans, ham salad, pork, beef.

Savory
Squash, peas, cauliflower, salads, chicken, turkey, lamb.

Chervil
Shellfish, fish, chicken.

Fenugreek leaves
Indian dishes, chicken, pork, vegetables, sausages.

Parsley
Eggs, beans, potatoes, shellfish, fish, chicken, pork, lamb, beef.

Tarragon
Eggs, vegetables, salads, beans, fish, chicken.

Chives
Eggs, sauces, salad, potatoes, lentils, chicken, beef.

Marjoram
Tomatoes, soups, beans, stuffings, chicken, lamb, beef.

Rosemary
Potatoes, squashes and other vegetables, stuffings, chicken, lamb, beef.

Thyme
Eggs, soups, potatoes, stuffings, casseroles, chicken, pork, sausages, lamb, beef.

STORE CUPBOARD

With a well-stocked store cupboard you can always rustle up a meal. These are my tried and tested favourites.

OILS AND VINEGARS
- Extra virgin olive oil
- Local rapeseed oil
- Vegetable oil

- Balsamic vinegar
- Cider vinegar
- Red wine vinegar
- White wine vinegar

CONDIMENTS
- English mustard powder
- Tomato ketchup
- Tabasco

- Tomato purée
- Soy sauce – light and dark
- Worcestershire sauce
- Fine sea salt
- Flaked sea sat
- Pink Himalayan sea salt
- Flavoured salt
- Black peppercorns
- White peppercorns

CANNED GOODS
- Anchovies
- Chickpeas
- Beans – different sorts such as haricot, kidney, butter beans
- Tomatoes (I prefer whole)

DRIED GOODS
- Couscous
- Dried beans
- Flour – plain, self-raising, wholewheat
- Ground almonds
- Lentils
- Nuts
- Pasta (range of types)
- Quinoa, bulgur, pearl barley
- Rice – basmati, risotto, wild, etc
- Sugar - golden caster sugar, demerara and brown sugar such as muscovado

JARS
- Capers
- Mayonnaise
- Tahini

SPICES
(These tend to go off after about a year and the flavour deteriorates. Keep an eye on them and replace as necessary.)
- Cayenne pepper
- Cinnamon sticks
- Coriander – seeds and ground
- Cumin – seeds and ground
- Curry powder
- Garam masala

- Ground ginger
- Nutmeg (whole)
- Smoked paprika (sweet and hot)
- Vanilla extract
- Vanilla pods and/or vanilla paste

EQUIPMENT

You don't have to have loads of fancy gadgets in your kitchen in order to produce great food. The real essentials are a good set of knives, sturdy pots and pans and a good chopping board. But the following is a list of what I feel a well-equipped kitchen should have. I advise building up your collection slowly and buying the best you can afford – particularly when it comes to knives and saucepans. They will repay you by lasting for years. Keep your knives well sharpened and store them in a knife block or on a magnetic strip on the wall.

KNIVES
- Boning knife
- Carving knife
- Cook's knife
- Flexible filleting knife for fish
- Paring knife
- Serrated knife
- Sharpener

POTS AND PANS
- A few good heavy-based saucepans (I favour stainless steel)
- Casserole dish
- Dutch oven – wonderful shape and you can cook anything in it
- Non-stick frying pan
- Small non-stick pan
- Steamer
- Tall stockpot

TINS AND DISHES
- Cake tins in a few sizes
- Baking trays and flat baking sheets with no sides

- Gratin dishes in a few sizes
- Loaf tins of 450g and 900g
- Mixing bowls
- Pyrex dishes
- Silicone baking mat
- Sturdy roasting tin
- Tart rings
- Tart tins of 20cm and 23cm

TOOLS AND UTENSILS
- Balloon whisk
- Digital meat thermometer
- Fine chinois (conical) sieve
- Flexible spatula
- Good potato peeler
- Kitchen scales
- Kitchen timer
- Large metal spoon for folding cake mixes

- Large pestle and mortar
- Lemon squeezer
- Mandolin slicer
- Measuring jug
- Measuring spoons
- Metal spatula
- Microplane grater
- Potato ricer and/or masher
- Salad spinner
- Scissors
- Tongs
- Wire rack

GADGETS
- Blender
- Electric hand mixer – get a good one
- Electric spice/coffee grinder
- Food processor

OVEN TEMPERATURES

We've given oven temperatures in recipes where appropriate but no two ovens are quite the same, so be prepared to use your judgement on cooking times. I do find a digital meat thermometer an invaluable tool for checking the internal temperature. If you would like Fahrenheit temperatures, see the chart below.

°C	Fan°C	Gas mark	°F
110°C	90°C	¼	225°F
120°C	100°C	½	250°F
140°C	120°C	1	275°F
150°C	130°C	2	300°F
160°C	140°C	3	325°F
180°C	160°C	4	350°F
190°C	170°C	5	375°F
200°C	180°C	6	400°F
220°C	200°C	7	425°F
230°C	210°C	8	450°F
240°C	220°C	9	475°F

WHAT'S IN SEASON

Below is a guide to when some popular vegetables and fruits are at their best in Britain. Obviously many are flown in from other countries so are available at other times and a few such as cabbage, pak choi, potatoes and bananas are in the shops all year round.

JANUARY

Vegetables: beetroot, Brussels sprouts, cauliflower, celeriac, celery, Jerusalem artichokes, kale, leeks, parsnips, purple-sprouting broccoli, salsify, swede, sweet potatoes, turnips.

Fruit: apples, clementines, grapefruit, oranges, pears, rhubarb.

FEBRUARY

Vegetables: Brussels sprouts, cauliflower, celeriac, celery, Jerusalem artichokes, kale, leeks, parsnips, purple-sprouting broccoli, swede, sweet potatoes, turnips.

Fruit: apples, clementines, grapefruit, lemons, oranges, rhubarb.

MARCH

Vegetables: Brussels sprouts, cauliflower, celeriac, Jerusalem artichokes, leeks, parsnips, purple-sprouting broccoli, spinach, spring greens, sweet potatoes, watercress.

Fruit: grapefruit, lemons, oranges, rhubarb.

APRIL

Vegetables: asparagus, cauliflower, celeriac, new potatoes, peas, purple-sprouting broccoli, spinach, spring greens, watercress.

Fruit: grapefruit, rhubarb.

MAY

Vegetables: asparagus, carrots, globe artichokes, new potatoes, peas, spinach, spring greens, tomatoes, watercress.

Fruit: apricots, grapefruit, nectarines, rhubarb, strawberries.

JUNE

Vegetables: asparagus, aubergines, broad beans, carrots, courgettes, fennel, garlic, globe artichokes, mangetout, new potatoes, peas, runner beans, spinach, spring greens, tomatoes, watercress.

Fruit: apricots, blackcurrants, cherries, gooseberries, nectarines, raspberries, redcurrants, rhubarb, strawberries, watermelon.

12

JULY

Vegetables: asparagus, aubergines, basil, beetroot, broad beans, broccoli, carrots, celery, courgettes, fennel, garlic, globe artichokes, mangetout, marrow, new potatoes, peas, runner beans, samphire, spinach, Swiss chard, tomatoes, watercress.

Fruit: apricots, blackcurrants, cherries, gooseberries, nectarines, peaches, raspberries, redcurrants, strawberries, watermelon.

AUGUST

Vegetables: aubergines, beetroot, broad beans, broccoli, carrots, celery, courgettes, fennel, garlic, globe artichokes, mangetout, marrow, peas, runner beans, samphire, spinach, sweetcorn, Swiss chard, tomatoes, watercress.

Fruit: apricots, blackberries, elderberries, figs, gooseberries, nectarines, raspberries, redcurrants, strawberries, watermelon.

SEPTEMBER

Vegetables: aubergines, carrots, celery, courgettes, fennel, garlic, globe artichokes, marrow, peas, pumpkin, runner beans, spinach, sweetcorn, Swiss chard, tomatoes, watercress.

Fruit: apples, apricots, blackberries, damsons, elderberries, figs, gooseberries, nectarines, peaches, pears, plums, raspberries, redcurrants, strawberries.

13

OCTOBER

Vegetables: aubergines, beetroot, broccoli, Brussels sprouts, cavolo nero, celeriac, celery, garlic, globe artichokes, Jerusalem artichokes, kale, kohlrabi, leeks, parsnips, peas, pumpkin, runner beans, salsify, swede, sweet potatoes, Swiss chard, tomatoes, turnips.

Fruit: apples, blackberries, cranberries, dates, elderberries, figs, pears, plums, quince.

NOVEMBER

Vegetables: beetroot, Brussels sprouts, cavolo nero, celery, globe artichokes, Jerusalem artichokes, kale, kohlrabi, leeks, parsnips, pumpkin, salsify, swede, sweet potatoes, Swiss chard, turnips.

Fruit: apples, clementines, cranberries, dates, pears, quince.

DECEMBER

Vegetables: beetroot, Brussels sprouts, cauliflower, cavolo nero, celery, globe artichokes, Jerusalem artichokes, kale, leeks, parsnips, pumpkin, salsify, swede, sweet potatoes, turnips.

Fruit: apples, clementines, cranberries, dates, grapefruit, pears, quince.

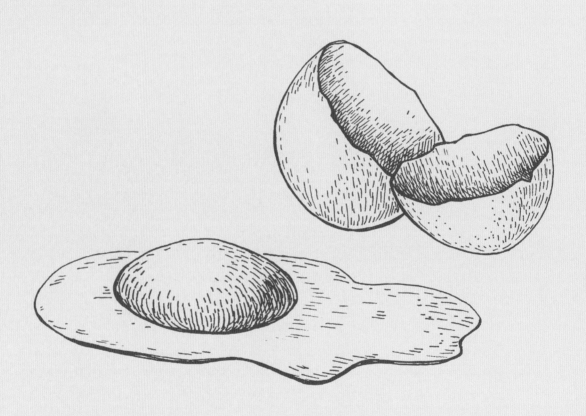

EGGS

*The chapter begins with the basics, then progresses, skill by skill,
recipe by recipe, up to showpiece dishes that really wow.*

I LOVE EGGS! They are packed full of protein, vitamins and minerals and I believe they are a number-one essential in any kitchen. They're also some of the first things many people learn to cook. Eggs are a meal in themselves – there's nothing I enjoy more than an omelette for a quick supper – and they are a vital part of so many dishes from sauces to cakes. In this chapter I take you through the preparation of these little packages of goodness from perfect boiled and poached eggs to beautiful soufflés.

People used to worry that eating eggs would increase their cholesterol levels, but now official NHS advice is that this is not a problem and we can eat as many eggs as we like.

Hen's eggs are far and away the most commonly used, but I also cook a lot of quail's eggs and I love to use duck eggs for cakes. They are higher in protein than hen's eggs and make richer cakes. Gull's eggs are a great delicacy – and expensive. They are available for just six weeks a year and only licensed collectors are allowed to gather them, and then only one egg from each nest. For an occasional treat, though, a soft-boiled gull's egg with hollandaise sauce takes a lot of beating.

I've also cooked ostrich eggs. When I took part in the TV programme *I'm a Celebrity . . . Get Me Out of Here!* I cooked a huge omelette for the gang using a 1.5kg ostrich egg!

But the bulk of the advice that follows is about hen's eggs and how to get the best from them.

FREE RANGE
Personally, I prefer not to buy eggs from caged birds, even though in the UK the old battery-style cages have been replaced by larger enclosures. Eggs labelled barn-reared also come from chickens that are kept indoors.

Free-range hens must have daytime access to outdoor runs and there are limits on how many birds can be kept in each enclosure. They are fed better food than the caged birds so their eggs taste good and have rich golden yolks.

However, free-range standards do vary and not all free-range producers are beyond reproach. If you want to be sure about the conditions your eggs are produced in, buy from a local supplier that you know is good and reliable, or choose organic eggs certified by the Soil Association. These eggs are laid by hens that are properly free-range, with more space per bird, and there are stricter limits on how many birds can be kept together. The hens are fed an organic diet and kept on organic land.

FRESHNESS
If you are lucky enough to sample day-old eggs they are superb, but unless you keep your own hens that's rarely possible. The way to judge the freshness of an egg is to put it in a bowl of water. If it sinks to the bottom it is good and fresh. If it sinks halfway it is reasonable, but if the egg floats it is past its best.

STORAGE

I don't keep my eggs in the fridge as they are best used at room temperature. But I do check the use-by date on the box and I would not want to eat an egg that's past this date. I don't like waste so I prefer to buy my eggs as I need them to be sure they are fresh. Find a good source that you can rely on and stick with it.

Eggs past their sell-by date might not be off, but if, for example, you boil an old egg the yolk will be rubbery. A sure sign of an old egg is that the shell is harder to take off. The fresher the egg, the easier it is to remove the shell.

Bear in mind that egg shells are porous and hence eggs absorb flavour through their shells. This can be a good thing. To give you an extravagant example, if you put a truffle into your box of eggs they take on that wonderful aroma. But you wouldn't want garlic-flavoured eggs in your crème caramel!

SIZE AND WEIGHT

I use large eggs in my recipes, unless otherwise stated, but it is useful to know the average weights of hen's eggs. These are the weights of shelled eggs.

- **Small:** 43–53g
- **Medium:** 53–63g
- **Large:** 63–73g
- **Very large:** 73–80g

EGG WHITES

Egg whites freeze beautifully so if you're making something that requires lots of yolks such as Crème Brûlée (see page 216), freeze the egg whites for another time. Defrost them in the fridge overnight before using them.

The most important thing when whisking egg whites is to have a scrupulously clean bowl and whisk. There mustn't be a single drop of oil or wetness on your equipment or the eggs won't beat properly. I like to use a stainless-steel bowl as it stays nice and cold, but glass is fine too.

Separate the eggs carefully and make sure no yolk finds its way into the bowl. Start whisking with a balloon whisk or an electric hand mixer and continue until the egg whites are opaque in colour, smooth and form firm peaks on the whisk. Then STOP. If you overwork the whites and go on whisking for too long they will start to split and become watery.

For sweet eggs, you can add a little sugar once they reach soft peak stage as that will help to stabilise the mixture. With savoury eggs, I sometimes add a little raspberry vinegar once whipped to soft-peak stage, for the same reason.

EGG YOLKS

Egg yolks don't freeze well, but you can keep them in the fridge for a day or two if necessary. It is vital to keep egg yolks covered – you can't leave them exposed to the air or they dry out and an unpleasant skin forms over them. Put the egg yolks in a bowl and place cling film over the surface so there is no air between the egg and the film.

♟ COOK'S TIP ♟

I do enjoy quail's eggs, though peeling them can be a faff. The easy way is to knock the pointed end on a hard surface, then put your thumb in and get under the membrane of the shell. Then continue spiralling round and round until you get to the bottom of the egg, then carefully pull off the shell. You'll find that with practice you will be able to remove the shell in one piece.

THE PERFECT BOILED EGG

A perfect boiled egg is a thing of beauty. You might think that
everyone knows how to boil an egg, but you'd be surprised!
Here's how to get your boiled eggs just right.

SERVES 1

2 large fresh eggs
fine sea salt and
    black pepper

1 First of all, the eggs should be at room temperature.
  If they are too cold, they are more likely to crack
  when you add them to the water.

2 Bring a pan of water to a rolling boil, add the eggs
  and start timing – see timings below.

3 If you're making soft-boiled eggs, serve them straight
  away with salt and pepper. For hard-boiled eggs, put
  them into cold water to cool, but peel them while still
  warm – it's much easier.

Timings for large hen's eggs (for medium, reduce
timings by 1 minute):
- **Runny soft-boiled egg (to dip your soldiers in):**
  5 minutes
- **Not quite as runny:** 6 minutes
- **Egg that it is not quite set:** 7 minutes (ideal
  for putting on toast with lots of pepper and for
  Scotch eggs)
- **Softly set egg:** 8 minutes (great for salads)
- **Hard-boiled egg:** 10 minutes

Timings for quail's eggs
- **Soft:** 2 minutes, 16 seconds
- **Set:** 3 minutes
- **Hard:** 4 minutes

🍴 COOK'S TIP 🍴
Never boil eggs for longer than 10 minutes –
the yolks get dry and crumbly and are not nice.

THE PERFECT POACHED EGG

There are two ways to poach eggs. In the first method, the egg is cooked in
a shallow frying pan and the beautiful yolk remains visible. This is good for
poaching eggs to be served on toast or for topping dishes such as baked beans.

In the second method, the egg is cooked in a deep pan of water.
The water is swirled so the white wraps around the yolk and covers it.
This is the cheffy technique and is the way to poach eggs if preparing
them in advance – for example, for use in the soufflés on page 36.

SERVES 1

1 large fresh egg
2 tsp white wine vinegar
(for saucepan method)
fine sea salt and
black pepper

Frying pan method

1 Fill a frying pan three-quarters full with water and
bring the water to a simmer. The water should not
boil – this is most important. Crack the egg into a
cup and carefully pour it into the water. Leave it for
30 seconds, then take a spatula and gently loosen the
base of the egg from the pan if necessary.

2 Keep the water just simmering and spoon a little
water over the yolk. A large egg should cook in
2½ minutes. When the egg is ready, remove it with
a slotted spoon and put it on a cloth or some kitchen
paper to drain – otherwise you will have soggy toast!
Season with salt and pepper to taste.

Saucepan method

1 Bring a large pan of water to simmering point and
add the white wine vinegar.

2 Crack the egg into a cup. Use a large spoon to swirl
the water, creating a vortex, then pour the egg into
the centre. Keep the water swirling so the egg white
wraps around the yolk. For a really runny egg (or one
you are going to reheat), cook for 2 minutes. For a
slightly firmer egg, cook for 2½ minutes. Season with
salt and pepper to taste.

3 If poaching an egg in advance, remove it from the
pan and put it straight into a bowl of iced water.
You can keep the egg in the water in the fridge for
up to 3 days, changing the water every day. To reheat,
place the egg in a pan of simmering water for no
more than 30 seconds.

PLAIN OMELETTE

I think one of the nicest things to eat is a simple, freshly made omelette.
It's the quickest, most delicious meal and something I always
enjoy. It's not difficult – just follow this easy recipe.

SERVES 1

2 large or 3 medium eggs
25g butter
1 tbsp chopped parsley,
   to garnish
fine sea salt and
   black pepper

1 Lightly whisk the eggs in a bowl and season them
   well with salt and pepper.

2 Melt the butter in a small frying pan over a medium
   heat. Pour in the eggs, leave for a few seconds, then
   mix the eggs around carefully with a fork until they
   are just beginning to set. At this stage you can add
   any extras such as ham or cheese. Just sprinkle them
   on and mix once, keeping the middle still slightly
   runny.

3 While the omelette is still on the soft side, fold it
   over twice to the side of the frying pan and leave
   for 30 seconds. Flip the omelette on to a plate and
   sprinkle over the parsley to serve.

CHORIZO FRIED EGGS ON TOASTED SODA BREAD

Quick and tasty, this really hits the spot. It makes an excellent brunch dish, but I enjoy it at any time of day. Everything is cooked in one pan so the eggs pick up lots of lovely flavour from the spicy chorizo.

SERVES 4

2 tbsp rapeseed oil
   or olive oil
200g chorizo, cut into
   5mm rounds
1 tbsp chopped thyme
   leaves, plus some
   sprigs to garnish
4 large eggs
4 slices of good soda bread
30g butter (at room
   temperature)
100g Manchego cheese,
   finely grated
1 tsp flaked sea salt

1 Heat the oil in a frying pan over a medium heat. Add the chorizo and the thyme leaves and cook for about 2 minutes. Remove the chorizo with a slotted spoon, transfer it to a plate and cover with foil to keep it warm.

2 Put the frying pan with the chorizo-flavoured oil over a medium-high heat. Crack each egg into a cup and add it to the pan. Fry the eggs until the whites are cooked and the edges are crispy.

3 Meanwhile, lightly toast the soda bread on one side under a hot grill. Mash the butter and cheese together with a fork, then spread the mixture over the untoasted side of the bread.

4 Put the toasts under the grill for a minute to melt the cheese. Remove them and quickly top each piece with some chorizo and a fried egg. Garnish with sprigs of thyme, season with salt and serve at once.

MAYONNAISE

Mayonnaise is one of those basics that is always good to have in the fridge. The bought versions are fine but it actually takes very little time to make your own and that way you know exactly what's in it. This is a basic mayo to which you can add your own flavourings.

MAKES 300G

2 egg yolks
1 tsp English mustard
    powder
300ml sunflower oil
¾ tsp fine sea salt
juice of ½ lemon

1 Whisk the egg yolks and mustard powder together, making sure they are well combined. I find a balloon whisk gives the best results.

2 Start adding the oil very slowly, drop by drop at first. Once the mixture has homogenised, you can start pouring in the oil in a thin stream. Keep whisking all the time. If your mayonnaise starts to split, just add a little cold water. If that doesn't work, add another egg yolk.

3 Add the salt, then beat in the lemon juice. If you find the mayonnaise is getting too thick while you are adding the oil, you can add the lemon juice sooner.

4 If you're in a hurry you can use a food processor, but the mayo won't be quite as thick. Simply whizz the egg yolks and mustard together, then add the oil very slowly and proceed as above.

5 Store the mayonnaise in the fridge until needed. It will keep for 3 or 4 days. If you want to keep the mayonnaise for longer, add a film of sunflower oil on the top to preserve it. It should then keep for at least a week.

AIOLI MAYONNAISE

One of my favourite mayonnaises, this has a much stronger
flavour than the basic recipe opposite. It's great with fish soup,
cold meats or served as a dip with sticks of raw vegetables.

MAKES 250G

pinch of saffron threads
2 egg yolks
1 tsp English mustard
   powder
250ml extra virgin
   olive oil
juice of ½ lemon
1 garlic clove, peeled
   and finely grated
fine sea salt and
   white pepper

1 Mix the saffron threads with a teaspoon of just-boiled
   water in a small bowl.

2 Whisk the egg yolks and mustard together in another
   bowl, using a balloon whisk if possible. Make sure
   they are well combined.

3 Start adding the oil very slowly, drop by drop. If you
   find the mayonnaise is getting too thick, add half the
   lemon juice, then continue adding the oil.

4 Once you've added all the oil, stir in the saffron and
   water, mixing well to give the aioli a wonderful rich
   yellow colour throughout. If you haven't already
   added lemon juice, add some now or add more
   to taste.

5 Now add the finely grated garlic and mix well. I find
   one clove enough, but add more if you like. Season
   with salt and pepper.

🥄 COOK'S TIP 🥄
Before juicing a lemon, cut both ends
off and then cut the lemon in half. You
will find it much easier to squeeze.

SOFT-BOILED EGGS WITH CHIMICHURRI AND AVOCADO ON CIABATTA

Everyone seems to love crushed avocado and this is my favourite
way of serving it. I like avocado with something quite spicy, so
I think chimichurri – a classic South American herby sauce – is
perfect. This combination just works and it's delicious.

SERVES 4

2 avocados, peeled
    and stoned
zest and juice of 1 lime
3 tbsp olive oil
1 ciabatta loaf
1 garlic clove, peeled
    and finely chopped
4 large eggs (at room
    temperature)
fine sea salt and
    black pepper

Chimichurri sauce
2 long fresh red
    chillies, seeded and
    finely chopped
3 garlic cloves, peeled
    and finely chopped
2 large handfuls curly
    parsley, leaves
    only, chopped
4 heaped tsp dried
    oregano
2 tsp flaked sea salt
5 tbsp red wine vinegar
5 tbsp extra virgin
    olive oil

1 Start by making the chimichurri sauce. Place the chopped chillies in a bowl and add the remaining ingredients, plus 5 tablespoons of cold water. Stir until well combined, then set aside. I do like the texture of the handmade sauce, but if you are short of time, you can roughly chop the chillies, garlic and herbs in a food processor. Add the salt, vinegar, oil and water, and pulse – don't overwork the mixture or you will end up with a mush.

2 Put the avocado flesh in a large bowl. Add the lime zest and juice and a tablespoon of the olive oil. Mash with the back of a fork to a rough consistency. Season with salt and pepper.

3 Preheat the grill. Cut the ciabatta in half horizontally, and slice each piece across to make 4 square pieces. Mix the garlic with the remaining olive oil and drizzle this mixture over the cut sides of the ciabatta. Toast the bread under the grill until golden brown.

4 Place a pan of water on your hob and bring it to the boil. Gently lower the eggs into the water and bring the water back up to the boil. Cook for 5½ minutes, then drain and run them under cold water until they are just cool enough to peel.

5 To serve, place the toasted ciabatta on plates and divide the crushed avocado between them. Place an egg on each piece of bread and carefully cut the egg in half, then drizzle with the chimichurri sauce. Serve at once.

SMOKED PAPRIKA AND
CHARGRILLED RED PEPPER FRITTATA

Frittatas are the Italian version of omelettes and are simple to make.
I always used to cook a frittata for the family on a Sunday night, when
everyone was peckish but didn't want a big meal. This can also be cut
into small slices to serve as canapés or makes good picnic food.

SERVES 4–6

400g waxy potatoes,
   peeled and cut
   into 1cm dice
2 red peppers, cut in
   half and seeded
2 garlic cloves, peeled
   and chopped
extra virgin olive oil
1 Spanish onion, peeled
   and thinly sliced
1 rounded tsp sweet
   smoked paprika
1 tbsp chopped
   thyme leaves
6 eggs
2 tbsp chopped
   flatleaf parsley
flaked sea salt and
   black pepper

1 Bring a pan of salted water to the boil, add the diced
potatoes and cook until just done. Drain the potatoes
and set them aside.

2 Preheat the oven to 220°C/Fan 200°C/Gas 7. Put the
pepper halves in an ovenproof dish. Add the garlic
and drizzle with a tablespoon of oil, then put the dish
in the oven and cook for 30–40 minutes. Remove the
peppers and tip them into a bowl, then cover and
leave to cool. Peel the skin off the peppers and cut
the flesh into strips.

3 Heat 2 tablespoons of oil in a 25cm non-stick,
ovenproof frying pan. Add the onion and cook over
a medium-high heat until lightly browned. Add the
potatoes and cook until lightly browned on all sides.
Sprinkle with a teaspoon of salt and the smoked
paprika, then cover the pan. Continue to cook gently
for 5 minutes until the potatoes are completely
cooked through and the onions are very soft.
Add the red peppers and cook for 2 minutes.

4 Whisk the eggs in a bowl and season with salt and
pepper, then add the cooked onion and potato
mixture and the thyme. Pour the egg mixture into
the pan and shake the pan a little. Sprinkle over the
parsley and cook the frittata gently over a low heat
for about 7 minutes, or until the egg on the bottom
has set and browned. Then put the pan under a low
grill and cook until the top of the frittata has set.
Alternatively, finish cooking the frittata in the oven
preheated to 200°C/Fan 180°C/Gas 6 for 3–4 minutes.

5 Slide the cooked frittata on to a board or plate and
serve hot or cold.

YORKSHIRE PUDDINGS

When I was chef at Amhuinnsuidhe Castle on the Isle of Harris in Scotland, we used to cook roast beef and Yorkshire puddings every Sunday. Problem was that every time we cooked the Yorkshires in a scalding-hot oven, we set off the fire alarms. In the end, we used to ring the fire department in advance and warn them! Yorkshire puddings are real comfort food and these are beautifully light. There's nothing better than a roast with Yorkshires.

MAKES 6

120g plain flour
1 tsp fine sea salt
180g eggs (shelled –
    about 3 large eggs)
180ml whole milk
100ml dripping or
    sunflower oil

1 Mix the flour and salt together in a large bowl. Make a well in the centre, crack in the eggs and mix well. Gradually add the milk and beat the mixture until smooth. Cover the bowl and leave the batter to rest for an hour if possible. Preheat the oven to 240°C/Fan 220°C/Gas 9.

2 Pour the dripping or oil into 6 individual Yorkshire pudding tins and put the tins into the preheated oven to heat until the fat is sizzling hot. Remove carefully, pour in the batter and immediately put the tins back in the oven. Cook the Yorkshires for about 15 minutes until puffed up and golden. Serve at once.

♥ COOK'S TIP ♥

You can make these in advance and heat them up in the oven at the last minute. And if you prefer to make one big Yorkshire pudding, preheat the oven to 240°C/Fan 220°C/Gas 9. Cook the pudding for about 15 minutes, then turn the temperature down to 200°C/Fan 180°C/Gas 6 and cook for another 15–20 minutes. If the top starts to get too brown, cover it with foil.

HOLLANDAISE SAUCE

This delicious sauce can be served with eggs, fish, chicken and vegetables such as asparagus. It is cooked in a bain-marie – a bowl sitting over a pan of simmering water. This helps ensure that the heat is gentle, reducing the risk of the sauce curdling. For this sauce you need clarified butter. This simply means removing the milk solids, as described below, to give a clear yellow fat that can be heated to a higher temperature without burning.

MAKES 250ML

250g unsalted butter
1 tbsp white wine vinegar
4 medium egg yolks
juice of 1 lemon
fine sea salt

1 To clarify the butter, put it in a small pan and heat it very slowly until melted. When the butter starts to foam slightly, remove the pan from the heat and leave it to stand for a few minutes to allow the milky white solids to sink to the bottom. Carefully pour the clear butter into a jug and discard the solids.

2 Place the vinegar and the egg yolks in a heatproof bowl that fits over a small pan. Bring some water to a simmer in the pan, then place the bowl over the top – the base of the bowl shouldn't touch the water.

3 Over a low heat, whisk the egg yolks continuously until they have a slightly thicker consistency. Be careful not to overheat the eggs or they will scramble.

4 Remove the pan from the heat and add the clarified butter, a little at a time, whisking constantly until the mixture is emulsified. If it is too thick at this stage, add a few drops of water until you are happy with the consistency. Finally, stir in the lemon juice to taste and season with salt and serve immediately. (If you like, you can use a tablespoon of Noilly Prat vermouth instead of lemon juice.)

Variations
You can flavour your hollandaise in a number of ways.
- **Mild mustard sauce:** add 2 tablespoons of Dijon mustard with the lemon juice
- **Mousseline sauce:** fold in 100ml whipped double cream just before serving
- **Ginger sauce:** add a tablespoon of ginger syrup from a jar of stem ginger just before serving
- **Mint hollandaise:** add 2 tablespoons of finely chopped mint just before serving

BÉARNAISE SAUCE

Béarnaise is a classic French sauce, traditionally served with steak.
Like hollandaise, it is cooked in a bain-marie – a bowl sitting over
a pan of simmering water – and is made with clarified butter.

MAKES 250ML

250g unsalted butter
6 tbsp white wine vinegar
2 shallots, peeled and
    finely chopped
6 black peppercorns,
    crushed
4 medium egg yolks
juice of ½ lemon
4 tbsp chopped
    tarragon leaves
fine sea salt

1 To clarify the butter, put it in a small pan and heat
   very slowly until melted. When the butter starts
   to foam slightly, remove the pan from the heat and
   leave it to stand for a few minutes to allow the milky
   white solids to sink to the bottom. Carefully pour
   the clear butter into a jug and discard the solids.

2 Rinse out the pan and add the vinegar, shallots and
   crushed peppercorns. Simmer for 1 minute to reduce
   the vinegar.

3 Find a heatproof bowl that fits neatly over a pan
   of water – the base of the bowl shouldn't touch the
   water. Pour the reduced vinegar into the bowl and
   add the egg yolks. Bring the water in the pan to a
   simmer, then turn the heat down. Keeping the heat
   low, whisk the vinegar and eggs continuously until
   they thicken. Take care not to overheat or the eggs
   will scramble.

4 Remove the pan from the heat and add the clarified
   butter, little by little, whisking constantly until the
   sauce is emulsified. If it seems too thick at this stage,
   add a few drops of water until you are happy with
   the consistency. Finally, stir in the lemon juice and
   tarragon to taste and season with salt.

BLACK PUDDING, LAMB AND MINT SCOTCH EGGS

I've adored black pudding ever since I worked in Scotland and used to get the best ever from Stornoway. I find it goes particularly well with lamb and this recipe is delicious. It does take a bit of work but there's nothing difficult, so just get organised and work methodically and you'll have a dish to be proud of. By the way, no pepper needed as black pudding is quite peppery already.

MAKES 8

8 quail's eggs
180g lamb mince
90g black pudding, diced
10 mint leaves,
    finely chopped
1 tsp fine sea salt
150g plain flour
2 hen's eggs, beaten
200g panko breadcrumbs
vegetable oil, for
    deep-frying

1 Bring a small pan of water to the boil. Lower the quail's eggs into the water and cook them for 2½ minutes. Remove and immediately plunge the eggs into iced water to halt the cooking process. Peel them carefully and set aside.

2 Put the mince, black pudding and mint in a bowl and mix them together well. Season with the salt, divide the mixture into 8 equal portions, then flatten the portions out slightly. Wrap each portion around a peeled quail's egg, using your hands to form an even coating.

3 Place the flour, beaten eggs and breadcrumbs into 3 separate bowls. Roll each covered egg in the flour, tapping off any excess or the beaten egg won't stick properly. Place it in the beaten egg, then straight into the breadcrumbs, making sure there is a nice even coating. Repeat the process to double coat each egg.

4 Half fill a large pan or a deep-fat fryer with vegetable oil and heat the oil to 170°C. Preheat the oven to 170°C/Fan 150°C/Gas 3½.

5 Add half the Scotch eggs to the hot oil and deep-fry for 5–6 minutes until golden brown and crisp. Remove them with a slotted spoon, draining off any excess oil, and place them on a baking sheet. Fry the remaining eggs in the same way, then bake them in the oven for 4 minutes to make sure all the meat is cooked through. Serve the eggs right away while they are still hot.

SPINACH SOUFFLÉS WITH POACHED EGGS

Everyone is a bit nervous of making soufflés, but I promise
you can't go wrong with this one. It is so delicious and has the
surprise of the poached egg in the middle! This is a good recipe for
showing off your cookery skills without being too difficult.

SERVES 4

Spinach
20g salted butter
250g fresh baby
    spinach, washed

Poached eggs
2 tbsp white wine vinegar
4 eggs

Soufflé mixture
25g unsalted butter, plus
    extra for greasing
25g Parmesan cheese,
    finely grated
25g plain flour
100ml whole milk
75g Gruyère cheese,
    grated
2 egg yolks
5 egg whites
fine sea salt and
    white pepper

1 Melt the salted butter in a large pan over a medium
heat, then add the spinach and let it wilt for a couple
of minutes. Drain well, then pat the spinach dry with
a cloth. Put it into a blender and blend to a smooth
purée, then set aside.

2 Bring a pan of water to a simmer and add the
vinegar. Crack an egg into a cup. Making a swirl in
the water to create a vortex, pour the egg into the
centre and keep the swirling going so the egg white
wraps around itself. Cook for 2 minutes, then remove
the egg with a slotted spoon and put it in a bowl of
cold water to stop the cooking process. Repeat with
the remaining eggs. You can make these in advance
and keep them in a bowl of cold water in the fridge.

3 Preheat the oven to 210°C/Fan 190°C/Gas 6½. Grease
4 x 10cm soufflé dishes with butter. Sprinkle the
insides with some of the Parmesan, turning each dish
to coat the sides, then tip out any excess. This helps
the soufflé to lift away from the dish and rise.

4 Melt the 25g of unsalted butter in a small pan. Add
the flour and cook over a low heat for 30 seconds,
while stirring, without letting it brown. Gradually
pour in the milk, stirring constantly and making sure
there are no lumps. Bring the milk to a simmer and
cook gently for 1 minute. Add the puréed spinach,
folding it in well, and season with salt and pepper.

5 Remove the pan from the heat, add the Gruyère
cheese and stir until it has melted. Leave the mixture
until it is just warm, then add the egg yolks and mix
well. Put the egg whites in a large, very clean bowl
with a pinch of salt and whisk until they form soft
peaks. Roughly fold a third of the egg whites into the
soufflé mixture, then gently fold in the rest.

6 Put a large tablespoon of the mixture into each dish and top with a well-drained cold poached egg. Add another large spoonful of the mixture so the dishes are about three-quarters full and the eggs are completely covered. Run your finger around the rim of each dish – this will help the soufflés rise evenly.

7 Place the soufflés in the preheated oven and bake for 10–12 minutes. They are ready when they are well risen, firm around the edges but still soft and creamy in the centre. They should have a slight wobble. Sprinkle them with the remaining Parmesan.

8 Make sure everyone is ready and take the soufflés straight to the table to be admired in all their glory before they begin to fall.

SALADS

The chapter begins with the basics, then progresses, skill by skill, recipe by recipe, up to showpiece dishes that really wow.

I MAKE MYSELF A WONDERFUL SALAD EVERY DAY FOR LUNCH

and for me, salad does not only mean green side salads – lovely as they are. It's also about bringing together interesting combinations of fresh ingredients to make a tasty meal in a bowl that's healthy, sustaining and delicious. You can make a salad out of almost anything and I create new ones all the time.

As a refreshing accompaniment to a main meal you can't beat a green salad made with spanking fresh leaves. I do prefer to buy an assortment of leaves and mix them myself, rather than use the supermarket bags, and I do believe you get a much better result that way.

Buy what looks freshest and most delicious on the day. Then when you get home, spend a few moments picking the lettuces apart and discard any damaged or wilted leaves. Wash them well in cold water, then dry them thoroughly. A salad spinner is ideal for this or just wrap the leaves in a clean tea towel, go outside and hurl it round your head as though you're about to toss a caber! Always make sure your salad leaves are thoroughly dry or they won't hold the dressing properly.

Put the dried leaves in a plastic bowl, cover them with a damp tea towel and pop them in the fridge. Now you have a beautiful mixture of leaves all ready to go and you can grab a handful whenever you want. This is just as convenient as a bag of pre-prepared salad from the shops and much tastier and cheaper.

I like to add some fresh herbs to my green salads. Wash and dry them, roll them in kitchen paper, then in some cling film and store them in the fridge. If your herbs start to look a little limp, put them in a bowl of iced water and they will come alive and look fresh again.

It's important to season your salad leaves well before dressing for the best flavour. Add salt and pepper first, then toss the leaves with the dressing. And I never add tomatoes and cucumber to my green salad – I think they spoil the texture.

DRESSING

I like to make a fairly large quantity of my staple salad dressing (see page 43) and put it in a bottle with a screw top – or use a wine stopper. You don't want your basic dressing to be too dominant in flavour. I do use olive oil in many of my dressings, but I also like to use rapeseed oil, mixed with some sunflower oil.

I'm a big fan of rapeseed, as it is our native oil and it's produced in the UK. I also like using nut oils, such as walnut and hazelnut, but they are a luxury and need to be used with discretion, as most are quite strong tasting.

Once you have your basic dressing, you can add any extra ingredients that take your fancy – perhaps a little soy sauce if you're making a salad with Asian flavours, or some sesame seed oil, extra lemon juice or even ginger syrup from a jar of stem ginger. Spices, such as cumin or saffron, are also good, or perhaps a little grated fresh root ginger to add zing. Just decant some of your basic dressing into a jug and then mix in the extra ingredients. Keep tasting until you have a flavour you like.

SALAD LEAVES

There's such a great selection of salad leaves available now. Here are some of the ones I like best.

British round lettuce

This is one of my favourites in the summer months and I love its gentle flavour. I like to keep the leaves whole in a salad.

Cos or Romaine

This is a good substantial lettuce. You may need to remove the stalks if they are tough.

Little Gems

These are among the most useful lettuces. I like them in a green salad, but I also enjoy them fried in a little butter or oil or braised with peas. They are good in soups too.

Radicchio

Like all the endives, radicchio has a slightly bitter taste, which I enjoy. It is particularly good seared and goes very well with sea bass. Escarole also has a touch of bitterness but works well with a sweet dressing.

Mizuna and Rocket

Both of these have a good strong flavour. I particularly enjoy wild rocket.

Iceberg

Iceberg leaves can be used as wraps for crispy duck and other filling. They add nice crunch and cut the calories!

Lollo rosso and oakleaf

Both these lettuces have good colour and add drama to your salad bowl. You do need to use them quickly though, as they don't keep as well as some lettuces.

Watercress

I love the delicious peppery taste of watercress and I enjoy it with oily fish and with new potatoes.

TOMATOES

The best tomatoes are the ones you grow yourself, picked while they're warm from the sun. Otherwise buy tomatoes as you need them and try not to keep them too long, as they tend to go soggy. Always serve tomatoes at room temperature, never cold from the fridge – chilled tomatoes are tasteless. And they do need to be seasoned really well with lots of salt and pepper. Then I dress them with olive oil and perhaps a little garlic.

It's not always easy to find good tomatoes that really taste like tomatoes should. At Hadlow College we have planted 50 different varieties of tomato in an effort to come up with the sweetest and most interesting flavours.

SALAD AS A MEAL

If you're having a salad as a meal you need more than leaves. They give lightness, freshness and texture, but you need to add something more substantial such as leftover pasta, beans or lentils. Roasted squash is lovely in a salad, as are nuts and seeds for some delicious crunch. Avocado makes an excellent addition or you can throw in a few olives. One of my favourite tricks is to sprinkle some crumbled feta cheese over my salad for a zap of flavour. It's a strong-tasting cheese, so you only need a little.

When you're composing your salad, think freshness, texture and bulk. Have a look at my recipes on the following pages, then let your imagination take over and come up with your own great salads.

THE PERFECT GREEN SALAD

For me, a perfect green salad is made up of several different types of leaves
for a mixture of colours and textures, some fresh herbs and – most important –
a good, flavoursome dressing. I usually make a large batch of dressing and keep
it in the fridge. It will last for several weeks. Little Gems are good all-purpose
lettuces and lovely in salads or they can be fried in butter or oil, or braised. I love
the British round lettuce in summer when it has so much flavour. Then there
is peppery rocket, and colourful leaves such as lollo rosso and oakleaf. Other
varieties are crisp iceberg, cos or romaine and bitter leaves such as radicchio.
I prefer to buy whole lettuces rather than bags of salad leaves – the bags are
convenient if you are going to use them right away but they don't keep well.

SERVES 4

3 or 4 different types
   of lettuce
fresh herbs, such as
   chervil, coriander,
   flatleaf parsley
fine sea salt and
   black pepper

Dressing
2 tsp Dijon mustard
2 tbsp cider vinegar
2 tbsp lemon juice
1 tsp caster sugar
150ml extra virgin
   olive oil
150ml sunflower oil
1 tsp fine sea salt
1 tsp white pepper

1 Separate the leaves of the lettuces, wash them in
a sink of cold water, then dry them well in a salad
spinner. It's essential to get the leaves properly
dry or your lovely dressing won't coat the leaves
properly. If you're washing the leaves in advance,
wrap them in a damp cloth and store them in the
drawer at the bottom of the fridge.

2 When you're ready to make your salad, put the
washed and dried leaves in a serving bowl. Soft
lettuce can bruise easily, so it's better to tear the
leaves, if necessary, rather than cut them. Wash
and dry whichever herbs you're using and add
those to the bowl too. Now season the leaves
with salt and pepper – it is important to season
the salad as well as the dressing.

3 For the dressing, put the mustard in a blender with
the vinegar, lemon juice and sugar and pulse to
combine. With the motor running, add the oils in
a steady stream. Season with the salt and pepper,
then pour the dressing into a serving jug. You can,
of course, also make the dressing by hand, if you
prefer, using a whisk.

4 Add a little dressing to the salad and toss, then serve
the rest separately. You can add extra flavours to the
dressing if you like, such as soy sauce, lime juice,
garlic, chilli – whatever you fancy.

CHERRY TOMATO, RED ONION AND OREGANO SALAD

Tomatoes are available all year round, but they really are seasonal produce, best in the summer months. There's a huge range of different types, all varying in taste and sweetness, so be prepared to adjust your seasoning accordingly. Some need more salt and sugar than others. Always serve tomato salads at room temperature for the best flavour – never fridge-cold.

SERVES 4

500g mixed cherry
   tomatoes, halved
½ red onion, peeled
   and finely sliced
1 garlic clove, peeled
   and finely sliced
2 oregano sprigs, leaves
   only, to garnish
fine sea salt and
   black pepper

Dressing
½ tsp Dijon mustard
2 tbsp balsamic vinegar
75ml extra virgin olive oil
75ml rapeseed oil
squeeze of fresh
   lemon juice
1 tsp dried oregano
1 tsp caster sugar

1 First make the dressing. Stir the mustard and vinegar together in a small bowl, then whisk in the oils and keep whisking until the mixture emulsifies. Add the lemon juice, oregano and sugar, then season with salt and pepper to taste.

2 Put the tomatoes in a bowl, then add the red onion and garlic. Season with salt and pepper and mix everything together well. Leave the salad to stand for 20 minutes to allow the flavours to infuse.

3 When you're ready to serve, add 2 tablespoons of the dressing to the tomatoes and mix, then garnish with the oregano leaves. Take the rest of the dressing to the table so everyone can add more if they like.

CHICORY, HERB, ALMOND AND POMEGRANATE SALAD

Chicory, also known as endive, is at its best in early spring.
Its slightly bitter tang partners beautifully with some sweet
ingredients, such as pomegranate seeds, to make a delicious salad.

SERVES 4–6

40g flaked or slivered
 almonds
1 pomegranate
2 Little Gem lettuces,
 roughly torn
1 head of chicory,
 cut into slices
30g fresh coriander,
 leaves only, roughly
 chopped
30g flatleaf parsley,
 roughly chopped
2 marjoram sprigs,
 leaves only
30g basil leaves,
 roughly torn
8 large chervil sprigs
10g tarragon leaves

Dressing
1 tsp Dijon mustard
2 tsp white wine vinegar
50ml extra virgin olive oil
100ml rapeseed oil
squeeze of fresh
 lemon juice
pinch of caster sugar
fine sea salt and
 black pepper

1 First make the dressing. Stir the mustard and vinegar together in a bowl, then whisk in the oils and keep whisking until the mixture emulsifies. Add the lemon juice and sugar, then season with salt and pepper to taste and set aside.

2 Toast the almonds in a dry pan for a few moments over a medium heat until golden, keeping a close eye on them so they don't burn. Cut the pomegranate in half. Hold one half over a bowl, cut side down, and give it a good bang with a wooden spoon to release the seeds and juice. Repeat with the other half.

3 Put the lettuces, chicory and herbs in a large bowl. Just before serving, season the leaves with salt and pepper, then add one-third of the dressing and toss lightly. Add half the pomegranate seeds, some of the juice and the toasted almonds and mix well. Sprinkle the rest of the pomegranate seeds and almonds over the salad and serve immediately. Serve the rest of the dressing in a bowl or jug so people can help themselves.

47

SALADS

FRENCH BEAN SALAD WITH GARLIC AND BLACK PEPPER

This is one of my favourite salads – easy to do and as it keeps in the fridge for a couple of days it's worth making a good quantity. It goes well with almost anything, but I particularly enjoy it with barbecue food. Plenty of black pepper is essential, so be generous with the seasoning. Good warm or cold.

SERVES 4

450g fine French beans, topped and tailed
2 garlic cloves, peeled and crushed
2–3 tbsp best extra virgin olive oil
1 tsp flaked sea salt
good grinding of black pepper

1 Bring a pan of water to simmering point. Add the beans and cook them for 3 minutes – they should still be a little firm.

2 Drain the beans well and tip them into a bowl. While they are still warm, add the garlic, olive oil, salt and pepper and mix well.

> ♀ **COOK'S TIP** ♀
> I sometimes like to use smoked garlic in this salad to add another flavour dimension. And you can use any type of beans, such as bobby beans.

CAPONATA

You may be surprised to see cocoa powder in the ingredients list for this dish, but it is traditional in Sicily where caponata comes from. You only need a little cocoa powder but it really brings out the other flavours. This makes a lovely salad to serve on its own or as an accompaniment. The trick is not to let the aubergine get mushy. It needs to be soft but with some texture.

SERVES 4–6

100ml olive oil
2 medium aubergines, finely diced
½ large red onion, peeled and finely diced
2 celery sticks, finely diced
1 large courgette, finely diced
50g black olives, pitted and halved
2 tbsp capers, rinsed
20g caster sugar
25ml white wine vinegar
50g pine nuts
200g plum tomatoes, skinned and seeded
2 tbsp finely chopped parsley, to garnish
1 tbsp cocoa powder, to serve
fine sea salt and black pepper

1 Heat a tablespoon of the oil in a large frying pan and brown the aubergines until soft but not mushy. Do this in batches and don't overcrowd the pan, or the aubergines will steam and not brown. Remove each batch and set aside to drain on kitchen paper while you fry the rest, adding more oil when you need it.

2 Add another tablespoon of oil to the pan and cook the onion and celery until tender, but don't allow them to brown. Add the diced courgette and lightly brown it on all sides.

3 Put all the aubergines back into the pan and add the olives, capers, sugar, vinegar, pine nuts and tomatoes. Cook for about 10 minutes and be careful not to over-mix the ingredients – treat them gently.

4 Season the caponata with salt and pepper, sprinkle over the parsley and serve hot, warm or cold. Just before serving, dust with cocoa powder to enhance the flavours.

🥄 COOK'S TIP 🥄

To skin and seed tomatoes, put them in a pan of boiling water for 30 seconds. Remove them and put them in a bowl of cold water, then peel off the skins. They will come away easily. Cut the tomatoes into quarters, then cut out the seeds with a knife and discard.

HEIRLOOM TOMATO AND MOZZARELLA SALAD WITH PESTO

It's worth getting some good buffalo mozzarella for this salad and using a nice variety of heirloom tomatoes – you can get them in different colours now, which makes the salad so pretty and enticing. This recipe makes generous portions.

SERVES 4–6

1kg heirloom
    tomatoes, sliced
300g mozzarella cheese,
    torn into pieces (buffalo
    mozzarella is best)
3 tbsp extra virgin
    olive oil
2 tbsp aged balsamic
    vinegar
basil leaves, to garnish
fine sea salt and
    black pepper

Pesto
100g basil leaves
1 tsp flaked sea salt
1 garlic clove, peeled
    and crushed
30g pine nuts
40g Parmesan
    cheese, grated
150ml olive oil

1 First make the pesto – I do it the easy way. Simply put all the ingredients, except the oil, in a food processor. Blitz to a purée, then add the olive oil in a slow stream. Scoop the pesto into a bowl, season well with salt and pepper and set it aside.

2 Place the sliced tomatoes in a large bowl and add the mozzarella. Season with salt and pepper, then drizzle with the olive oil and mix gently.

3 Transfer the tomatoes and mozzarella to a serving dish and sprinkle with the balsamic. Drizzle the pesto over the top and garnish with basil leaves.

🥄 COOK'S TIP 🥄
You can age your own balsamic vinegar. Buy the cheapest bottle you can find and pour it into a pan. For 250ml of vinegar, add 2 heaped tablespoons of sugar and bring to the boil. Simmer until the consistency thickens and becomes syrupy, then cool and pour it back into the bottle. It's then ready to use!

MANGO, CARROT AND HAZELNUT SALAD

I ate lots of salads like this one when I spent time in Grenada.
My version is colourful and healthy, with a lovely Caribbean vibe.

SERVES 4

100g blanched hazelnuts
50g desiccated coconut
2 mangoes, ripe but still
    firm to the touch
1 carrot, peeled
    and grated
12 cherry tomatoes,
    halved
1 handful of watercress,
    leaves picked
    from the stems
flaked sea salt

Dressing
2 tbsp runny honey
1 tsp wholegrain mustard
juice and zest of 2 limes
6 tbsp extra virgin
    olive oil

1 For the dressing, whisk the honey, mustard, lime juice and zest and the olive oil in a small bowl until emulsified. Set it aside.

2 Toast the hazelnuts in a dry pan over a medium heat until golden. Tip them out on to a board, then crush them lightly. Toast the coconut in the dry pan until golden, shaking the pan regularly, then set it aside. Peel the mangoes, then slice off the flesh as close as possible to the stone and dice it.

3 Put the diced mango in a bowl with the grated carrot and add the tomatoes and watercress leaves. Gently mix everything together, taking care not to break up the mango too much.

4 Divide the salad between 4 plates or serve it in a bowl. Sprinkle over the toasted hazelnuts and coconut, then drizzle over the dressing and season with salt.

VEGETABLE NOODLE SALAD

Spiralising simply means cutting vegetables, such as carrots and courgettes, into thin ribbons. You could always do this with a julienne peeler, but a few years ago spiralising became all the rage and all sorts of special machines came on to the market. Some are good but others break all too quickly, so do your research if you're planning to invest in one. And remember that you can easily use a julienne or even just a potato peeler instead. The thing to remember is that the veg have to be really thin so they combine nicely with the dressing.

SERVES 4

2 carrots, peeled
2 courgettes
250g mangetout,
    finely sliced
4 radishes, thinly sliced
1 fresh red chilli, seeded
    and finely sliced
handful of coriander,
    roughly chopped
handful of mint,
    roughly chopped
fine sea salt and
    black pepper

Dressing
2 tbsp sesame oil
50g sesame seeds
1 garlic clove, peeled
    and finely chopped
1½ tsp soft brown sugar
1 tbsp fresh lime juice
2 tbsp light soy sauce

1 First make the dressing. Place the sesame oil and seeds in a small pan and set over a gentle heat. Keep stirring the seeds until they turn golden brown, then tip them into a small bowl and leave to cool.

2 Add the garlic, sugar, lime juice and soy sauce to the cooled, toasted seeds and whisk to make the dressing. Set aside.

3 Cut the carrots and courgettes into thin ribbons using a spiraliser, a julienne peeler or a potato peeler. Put them in a large bowl.

4 Add the mangetout, radishes and chilli to the bowl and drizzle over the dressing. Add salt and pepper to taste, then transfer to a serving dish and sprinkle with the coriander and mint.

PEAR AND BLUE CHEESE
WALDORF SALAD

Waldorf is a perfect winter salad but I'm happy to eat it all year round. Pears and blue cheese are such a delicious combination and this makes a good lunch or a lovely side dish with something like a seared chicken breast.

SERVES 4–6

2 ripe pears
juice of 1 lemon
¼ fennel bulb
150g seedless black
    grapes, halved
2 tbsp mayonnaise
1 tbsp crème fraîche
olive oil
2 celery sticks,
    finely sliced
60g walnut halves,
    roughly chopped
2 Little Gem lettuces
½ frisée salad
220g blue cheese
    (Yorkshire Blue, Kentish
    Blue and Stichelton are
    all good), crumbled
fine sea salt and
    black pepper

Garnish
good extra virgin olive oil
3 tbsp finely chopped dill

1 Peel and core the pears and chop them roughly. Put them in a bowl and mix with the lemon juice to stop them discolouring.

2 Cut the fennel into thin shavings, using a mandolin if you have one, and add the shavings to the bowl with the chopped pears. Toss the grapes with the pears and fennel.

3 In a large bowl, mix the mayonnaise, crème fraîche and a few drops of olive oil. Add the pears, fennel, grapes, celery, chopped walnuts and the lemon juice from the pear mixture, then season well with salt and pepper.

4 Chop the Little Gems into long strips and toss them at the last moment with the frisée and the blue cheese. Garnish with a few drops of extra virgin olive oil and the dill.

NEW POTATO SALAD WITH CHIVES AND SPINACH

Everyone loves a potato salad and I find you can never have enough.
Make sure you get good waxy potatoes that don't fall apart – Charlottes
work perfectly. This is such a simple salad but absolutely delicious.
It's fine to use bought mayo but it's even better with home-made.

SERVES 4

800g new potatoes,
    peeled or scraped
4 heaped tbsp mayonnaise
    (shop-bought or
    see page 24)
1 tsp Dijon mustard
juice of ½ lemon
1 tbsp extra virgin
    olive oil
150g baby spinach,
    leaves torn
20g chives, finely snipped
good pinch of paprika
    (optional)
fine sea salt and
    black pepper

1   I like to peel or scrape my salad potatoes, but you can just wash them well and leave the skins on if you prefer. Place the potatoes in a large pan with a pinch of salt and cover them with cold water. Bring to the boil, then turn the heat down to a simmer and cook for 15–20 minutes or until just cooked through. It is important not to over-boil the potatoes – you don't want mush! Drain the potatoes and leave them to cool to room temperature.

2   Slice the potatoes into halves or quarters, depending on their size. Place them in a large bowl. Mix the mayonnaise with the mustard and lemon juice, then add it to the bowl with the olive oil, spinach and chives. Season with salt and pepper, then mix well.

3   Transfer the salad to a serving dish and sprinkle with paprika, if using.

TARRAGON AND HAZELNUT QUINOA

A seed, not a grain, quinoa is gluten-free and packed with protein
so it's a really healthy option. Combined with nuts, herbs and kale,
it makes a beautifully substantial salad that both tastes good and
does you good. This also goes well with fish, chicken or meat.

SERVES 4–6

350g quinoa
50g blanched hazelnuts
3 tbsp extra virgin
   olive oil
zest of 1 orange
2 tbsp chopped tarragon
100g kale, tough stalks
   removed, finely sliced
1 garlic clove, peeled
   and finely chopped
handful of chopped
   flatleaf parsley,
   to garnish
fine sea salt

1 Rinse the quinoa and put it in a large pan. Cover it
with 350ml of water and bring to the boil. Reduce
the heat and simmer for 10–12 minutes, or until
the quinoa is tender.

2 Toast the hazelnuts in a dry pan over a medium
heat for a few moments until golden, then chop
them roughly and set aside.

3 Drain the quinoa if all the water hasn't been
absorbed and put it in a large mixing bowl.
Drizzle over 2 tablespoons of the olive oil and
season with salt. Mix in the toasted hazelnuts,
orange zest and tarragon.

4 Heat the remaining oil in a frying pan over a
medium heat until warm. Add the kale and stir-fry
for 1–2 minutes, adding the garlic after a minute.
Continue to fry until the kale is just tender, then
tip it into a serving bowl with the quinoa and stir
to combine. Garnish with the parsley and serve
immediately.

BULGUR WHEAT, POMEGRANATE AND BEETROOT SALAD

I love bulgur wheat and it goes beautifully with beetroot
in this hearty, colourful dish. I like this for lunch, or you
could serve smaller portions as a starter if you like.

SERVES 4–6

300g cooked beetroots
    (shop-bought or cook
    your own; see below)
200ml vegetable stock
1 tbsp runny honey
1 tbsp pomegranate
    molasses or
    maple syrup
100g bulgur wheat
100g pine nuts
1 pomegranate
75ml extra virgin olive oil
2 tbsp balsamic vinegar
juice of ½ lemon
handful of mint leaves
5 spring onions,
    finely sliced
fine sea salt and
    black pepper

1 Put half the beetroots in a food processor with the
vegetable stock, honey and pomegranate molasses
or maple syrup. Blitz to a purée, then pass the
mixture through a fine sieve to remove any lumps.

2 Put the bulgur wheat in a pan and add the beetroot
purée. Season with salt and pepper, place the pan over
a medium heat and bring to the boil. Immediately
remove the pan from the heat and tip the contents
into a bowl. Cover the bowl with cling film and set
it aside while you prepare the rest of the salad.

3 Put the pine nuts in a small dry frying pan and
toast them for a few minutes over a medium heat.
Keep stirring them or shaking the pan so they don't
burn, and don't take your eyes off them! Cut the
pomegranate in half. Hold one half over a bowl, cut
side down, and give it a good bang with a wooden
spoon to release the seeds. Repeat with the other half.

4 Cut the remaining beetroots into small dice and place
them in a bowl. Add the olive oil, vinegar, lemon
juice, mint, spring onions and toasted pine nuts, then
mix well and season with salt and pepper to taste.

5 Fluff up the bulgur wheat with a fork and add it to
the beetroot. Mix, transfer the salad to a serving
bowl, then add the pomegranate seeds.

🥄 COOK'S TIP 🥄

If you want to cook your own beetroots, first
cut off the leaves leaving short stalks. Put the
beets in a pan of water, bring to a simmer and
cook for about 25 minutes or until soft.

ROASTED MEDITERRANEAN VEGETABLES WITH PUY LENTILS AND GOATS' CHEESE

This is such a good salad and very easy to cook and serve. I enjoy this with those little fresh goats' cheeses – sublime! Just make sure you don't overcook the vegetables. They should be tender and succulent but not blackened or the dish won't look appealing.

SERVES 6

2 small red onions, peeled and cut into 3cm dice
1 courgette, cut into 3cm dice
1 red pepper, seeded and cut into 3cm dice
1 aubergine, cut into 3cm dice
8 cherry tomatoes
2 garlic cloves, crushed
2 tbsp olive oil
2 tbsp balsamic vinegar
1 tsp dried herbes de Provence
fine sea salt and black pepper

Lentils
1 tbsp vegetable oil
½ white onion, peeled and finely chopped
2 garlic cloves, peeled and finely chopped
1 thyme sprig, leaves finely chopped
150g Puy lentils
250ml vegetable stock

To serve
200g goats' cheese, crumbled
bunch of basil, leaves shredded

1 Preheat the oven to 220°C/Fan 200°C/Gas 7. Place the red onions, courgette, red pepper, aubergine, cherry tomatoes and crushed garlic in a large roasting tin. Make sure that the vegetables aren't too crowded or they will steam rather than roast. Drizzle them with the olive oil and balsamic vinegar, season with salt and pepper, then toss everything together thoroughly.

2 Place the roasting tin in the oven and roast the vegetables for about 20 minutes, then turn them and add the dried herbs. Cook for another 10–15 minutes until the veg are soft, golden brown and cooked through. You can do all this in advance if you like.

3 Meanwhile, cook the lentils. Heat the oil in a medium pan and add the chopped onion, garlic and thyme. Cook them gently over a medium heat for 2–3 minutes or until golden brown. Add the lentils and stock to the pan, then turn down the heat to a simmer and cook for 20–25 minutes or until the lentils are soft but not mushy. Remove the pan from the heat and drain off any excess liquid.

4 If necessary, warm the vegetables in the oven for a couple of minutes. Add them to the lentils and check the seasoning, adding more salt and pepper if needed.

5 Serve the lentils and vegetables in warm bowls and top each serving with crumbled goats' cheese and some shredded basil leaves.

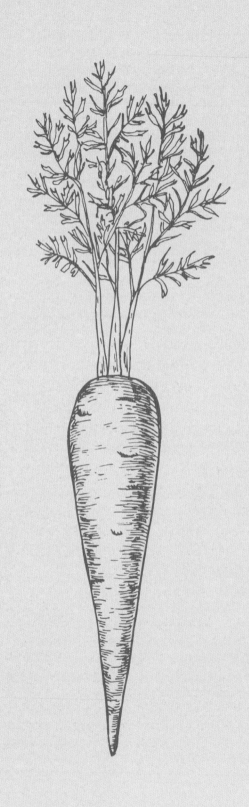

VEGETABLES

The chapter begins with the basics, then progresses, skill by skill, recipe by recipe, up to showpiece dishes that really wow.

THESE DAYS WE CAN GET ALMOST ANY VEGETABLE at any time of year. You'll find asparagus in the supermarkets in the depth of winter and parsnips in August. This can be confusing and I prefer to go to farmers' markets and pick up what's in season. Vegetables are always at their best – and cheapest – then. I enjoy the excitement of buying the earliest peas or the first of the autumn root vegetables. Have a look at my chart on pages 12–13 to see what's in season when.

More and more, I find myself regarding vegetables as a meal in themselves, not just as a garnish for meat and fish. They're an essential part of our diet, providing us with valuable fibre, minerals and vitamins, and we all know we should be eating at least five portions a day – more if possible. And if you prepare and cook your veg properly, this is certainly no penance.

PREPARING VEGETABLES

When you watch TV chefs preparing vegetables you may marvel at how quickly and easily they produce a pile of beautifully sliced onions or perfectly diced carrots. This takes experience, but with care and practice you can do an efficient job.

First of all, you need a sharp knife. Place the vegetable on a chopping board and hold it firmly with one hand, making sure your fingers are not in the way of the knife. With your other hand, hold the knife above the vegetable, with the point on the board. Push the knife down and forward into the vegetable, cutting as you go, then bring it up with a rocking movement to make the next cut. Try and lift the knife as little as possible between cuts.

- **Slicing onions** – first cut the onion in half through the root, then peel off the skin. Place one half on your board, cut side down, and slice it across as neatly as you can.
- **Slicing greens** – roll up the leaves tightly, then cut across to slice them into narrow ribbons.
- **Dicing** – slice the vegetable first, then cut it into cubes measuring about 1cm.
- **Matchsticks or julienne** – these are ideal for salads. Cut the vegetable into strips about 3mm thick.

COOKING VEGETABLES

It's not always easy to know the best way to cook different vegetables. When I did my time in the jungle in *I'm a Celebrity . . . Get Me Out of Here!* I found the meat we were presented with relatively easy to understand – after all, a leg is a leg whatever the beast. But I'd never come

COOK'S TIP

You often see the term 'blanched' for vegetables in recipes. This simply means to part-cook them. Root vegetables should be put into cold water and brought to the boil. Beans and shallots should be plunged into boiling water, then brought to the boil.

across some of the vegetables before, so I looked at their texture and density, tried to determine how much water they contained, then worked out the best way to cook them.

One of the easiest ways of cooking root vegetables is to put them in a gratin dish lined with foil, then add herbs, garlic and a bit of butter or oil and wrap them in the foil to make a parcel. You will keep all the natural juices of the vegetables and intensify the flavour – and you don't lose nutrients like you do when boiling vegetables in water.

I love roasting simple vegetables with lots of herbs and garlic – again, the flavour is intensified. Vegetables cooked this way make a good purée as well – just whizz them up in a blender.

Steamed vegetables are delicious, but choose carefully and season them well. Beans are good steamed, as are finely cut spring greens and cabbage. Root vegetables don't work so well.

Stir-frying is perfect for vegetables such as mangetout, peppers and pak choi and so quick to do. Root vegetables can also be stir-fried but parboil them first, unless you have cut them very small.

Vegetables such as asparagus, leeks and salsify are excellent cooked on a griddle pan and you get that lovely charred look. Pieces of butternut squash are also good cooked this way, as are French beans, but both need to be blanched beforehand. Aubergines can also be cooked on a griddle but they do need to be salted first to draw out the water, otherwise they soak up any oil like a sponge.

POTATOES
There are so many kinds of potatoes in the shops now and it can be difficult to know what to use for particular dishes. Opinions differ, but these are my preferences.
- **Roasting** – the flourier the better (unless roasting baby new potatoes). I like King Edward, Rooster and Salad Blue.
- **Mash** – King Edward, Maris Piper, Vivaldi.
- **Salads** – you need waxy potatoes such as Aya, Charlotte or Désirée.
- **Gratins** – Maris Piper, King Edward.
- **Sautéed** – Maris Piper, King Edward, Charlotte.

I also adore Jersey Royal potatoes, simply scraped, boiled with mint and served with butter. They are unique to the island of Jersey and many growers still use seaweed from the beaches as fertiliser. People say that this is what gives the potatoes their unique flavour. Jersey Royals have been granted Protected Designation of Origin (PDO) status and, unlike most potatoes, they have a definite season. They are harvested from March through to the end of July and are at their peak in May.

ORGANIC
I do enjoy organic vegetables and I certainly love to see some dirt on my carrots and potatoes, rather than buying them wrapped in plastic. But they are more expensive, and the important thing is to cook and enjoy plenty of vegetables, whether or not they are organic. Do wash all vegetables well before cooking.

CANNED AND FROZEN VEGETABLES
I always have some of these on hand – and I adore those canned French peas. They are a real treat. Canned tomatoes are a store-cupboard essential, but I do prefer to use the whole tomatoes in juice rather than the chopped variety, which I think taste tinny.

Frozen peas are wonderful – much better than frozen broad beans in my opinion – and frozen leaf spinach is excellent for use in soufflés or ravioli – be sure to drain it well. Frozen sweetcorn is good for fritters and soup, but I prefer to use canned for salads.

COOKING CARROTS

I adore carrots and their sweet flavour enhances so many dishes. They do deserve a little extra attention when cooked to serve on their own and they respond so well to the addition of herbs and spices. One of my favourite herbs for carrots is oregano. Start preparing your carrots by trimming the sides of each one to make it square so you can hold it steady. Then cut the carrots into batons, which can be any size you want but should be uniform, or into rounds.

Buttered carrots

Cut the carrots to the size you want and put them in a pan of boiling water with a little salt. Turn the heat down to a simmer and cook the carrots until they are tender but still have a little bite to them – al dente. Drain them well, then add some butter, a little more salt and some chopped parsley or coriander.

Spicy carrots

Cut the carrots to the size you want and put them in a pan. Add stock to cover, then spices such as star anise or nutmeg for extra flavour. Once the carrots are done, drain them well and remove the spices, then toss in some butter and season with salt and pepper.

Caramelised carrots

I like using Chantenay carrots for this. Put the washed whole carrots into a frying pan with a knob of butter and a tablespoon of oil. Cook them very slowly for 30–40 minutes until slightly caramelised, stirring them and moving them around regularly. Keep an eye on the carrots and add a little more oil if the pan starts to look dry. Add a spoonful of honey and continue to cook for another 5 minutes, then season with salt and pepper and serve.

ROASTED CARROTS WITH THYME, GARLIC AND OLIVE OIL

This is so easy and so good to eat. It makes a delicious side dish and you can cut the carrots into any shape you want or use baby carrots. Just be aware that the cooking time will vary slightly according to the size of your carrots.

SERVES 4

500g carrots, peeled and
   cut into whatever
   shape you like
40g butter
1 tbsp olive oil
3 whole garlic cloves,
   unpeeled
6 thyme sprigs or
   1 tsp dried thyme
good pinch of
   flaked sea salt

1 Preheat the oven to 200°C/Fan 180°C/Gas 6. Put a large piece of foil in a roasting tin. Add the carrots and the remaining ingredients and mix well.

2 Bring up the sides of the foil and seal the vegetables in the package. Put the tin in the oven and roast the carrots for 45 minutes.

3 Remove the tin from the oven and check that the carrots are tender. Leave the foil package open and put the carrots back in the oven for another 20 minutes until nicely browned. Check the seasoning, then tip them into a dish to serve.

69

CARROTS WITH GARLIC, TARRAGON AND ALMONDS

This is one of those dishes that goes with anything and is an excellent way of cooking carrots. I love crunchy food and cooking the carrots briefly, then adding toasted nuts, results in an excellent mix of textures and flavours.

SERVES 4

30g slivered or
   flaked almonds
400g carrots, peeled
   and cut into fine
   matchsticks or finely
   sliced into rounds
   on a mandolin
4 tbsp olive oil
1 garlic clove, peeled and
   very finely chopped
juice of 1 lemon
2 tbsp chopped tarragon
fine sea salt and
   white pepper

1 Toast the almonds in a dry frying pan over a medium heat for a couple of minutes until golden. Keep an eye on them so they don't burn.

2 Bring a pan of water to the boil. Add salt and the carrots, bring to the boil and cook for 1 minute. Drain well, then pat the carrots dry with kitchen paper.

3 While the carrots are still warm, add the olive oil and toss, then add the garlic, lemon juice, tarragon and most of the toasted almonds, reserving a few for the top. Season with salt and pepper, then toss again and garnish with the reserved almonds.

71

CUMIN-SPICED CAULIFLOWER

A seriously tasty dish and very quick to make, this uses one of my favourite spices, as cumin and cauliflower go together beautifully. This is good with grilled chicken or kebabs, perhaps with some minted yoghurt on the side.

SERVES 4–6

1 medium cauliflower
100g butter
1 tsp vegetable oil
3 tsp ground cumin
juice of ½ lemon
fine sea salt

1 Preheat the oven to 170°C/Fan 150°C/Gas 3½. Remove the leaves from the cauliflower and set them aside. Using a small sharp knife, cut the cauliflower into small florets about 3cm wide.

2 Heat the butter and oil in a large ovenproof frying pan – adding oil to the butter means that it won't burn so quickly. When the butter has melted, add the cumin and cook for 2 minutes to enhance the flavour. Add the cauliflower florets and leaves and the lemon juice to the pan and stir to coat all the florets in the spicy butter.

3 Place the pan in the preheated oven to cook for 20–25 minutes until the cauliflower is tender. Remove from the oven, season really well with salt and serve immediately. So delicious.

CAULIFLOWER COUSCOUS

I've called this cauliflower couscous because the little pieces of floret look rather like couscous. This makes wonderful diet food, as it provides loads of bulk and satisfaction but very few calories. It's very easy to prepare but you must have a super-fresh cauli with no brown bits.

SERVES 4

1 large cauliflower
75ml rapeseed oil
2 banana shallots, peeled
   and finely diced
4 tbsp finely chopped
   parsley
½ tsp sherry vinegar
fine sea salt and
   black pepper

1 Remove the leaves from the cauliflower, then separate into florets. Take each floret and slice down from the top of the stalk as finely as possible, then crumble the pieces with your fingers.

2 Pour the oil into a large pan and add the shallots. Cook over a low heat for 10 minutes until the shallots are soft and almost translucent but with very little colour. Add the cauliflower and parsley to the pan and cook gently for 1 minute, stirring all the time. The cauliflower should still have some bite to it.

3 When you are happy with the texture, season with sherry vinegar and some salt and pepper. The vinegar helps to cut through the fat in the oil and provides a bittersweet taste. Serve immediately.

CRUSHED NEW POTATOES

A real family favourite, buttery potatoes are always popular.
You don't need anything fancy here – regular new potatoes are fine
– and if you don't have the herbs, just add butter, oil and seasoning.
Recipes like this are guidelines for you to use and adapt as you like.

SERVES 4

500g new potatoes,
  washed
50g butter
3 tbsp extra virgin
  olive oil
4 spring onions,
  trimmed and sliced
1 tbsp chopped mint
2 tbsp chopped parsley
2 tbsp finely snipped
  chives
flaked sea salt and
  black pepper

1 Put the potatoes in a pan of cold water and add salt. Bring to the boil and boil for 15–20 minutes or until completely cooked through. To check, insert a small sharp knife into a potato. It should feel soft in the centre and the knife should pull out of the potato without any resistance.

2 Drain the potatoes in a colander and shake them vigorously to remove any excess moisture.

3 Tip the hot potatoes into a large warm bowl and immediately add the butter and olive oil. Using a potato masher or large metal spoon, crush the potatoes until they are broken up but not mashed. Stir in the spring onions and fresh herbs, then season to taste and serve immediately.

VEGETABLES

STIR-FRIED BRUSSELS SPROUTS WITH CHESTNUTS

I adore Brussels sprouts and I can't understand why so many people aren't keen on them. If you are one of those who aren't sure, try this recipe with bacon, chestnuts and butter and I bet you'll be converted. Lovely at Christmas. I think we need a campaign to get everyone eating sprouts again – they are delicious and good for you and deserve more attention.

SERVES 4

1 tbsp vegetable oil
50g pancetta, cut into matchsticks
2 banana shallots, peeled and sliced
2 garlic cloves, peeled and finely chopped
200g Brussels sprouts, trimmed and finely shredded
100g cooked chestnuts (vacuum-packed are fine), roughly chopped
25g butter
fine sea salt and black pepper

1   Heat the vegetable oil in a large frying pan and add the pancetta. Fry it over a high heat for 2–3 minutes until it's all crisp and golden brown.

2   Turn the heat down and add the shallots and garlic to the pan. Fry them for 2 minutes or until the shallots have browned.

3   Stir the Brussels sprouts, chestnuts and butter into the pan, then add 100ml of water. Cook over a high heat until the sprouts are tender but still al dente and all the water has evaporated. Add salt and pepper to taste and serve immediately.

BROAD BEAN, LIME, MINT AND CHILLI HOUMOUS

I know some people will be up in arms at me calling this a houmous, but it is the best way to describe it and it does contain chickpeas. Serve as a dip – perhaps with some home-made crisps (see page 87) or with sticks of raw vegetables. It keeps for about a week in the fridge if topped with olive oil.

SERVES 4

400g fresh broad beans, podded weight
120g canned chickpeas, drained (about half a can)
2 garlic cloves, peeled and crushed
zest and juice of 1 lime, plus extra juice if needed
pinch of ground cumin
100g crème fraîche
3 tbsp extra virgin olive oil, plus extra if needed
1 fresh red chilli, seeded and finely chopped
10 mint leaves, finely sliced
fine sea salt

1 Bring a pan of water to the boil, season with salt and cook the broad beans for 3 minutes or until tender. Drain them in a colander and then rinse them under cold running water until they are cool enough to handle but not cold – it's easier to remove the skins while the beans are still warm. Remove the greyish outer skins, then place the beans in a bowl of iced water. This stops them going brown. Once the broad beans are completely cold, drain them and pat dry with some kitchen paper.

2 Place the cooked beans in a food processor with the chickpeas, crushed garlic, lime zest and juice, cumin, crème fraîche and olive oil. Blend until smooth, adding more olive oil if the mixture seems too thick.

3 Spoon the houmous into a bowl. Stir in the chilli and mint. Taste for seasoning and add salt and extra lime juice if needed. Serve straight away or cover with olive oil to stop the houmous from discolouring if serving later.

♀ COOK'S TIP ♀
You can use frozen broad beans for this if you like, but you will still have to remove the skins.

AUBERGINE MOUTABAL

I visited Petra in Jordan a few years ago and while I was there, I spent a day at a cookery school where I tasted this wonderful dish. Stuffing the garlic into the aubergine in this way stops it from burning and going bitter, and the flavour is sublime. This is great served hot as a purée or cold as a dip with crudités.

SERVES 4

2 aubergines
4 garlic cloves, peeled and finely sliced
4 tbsp extra virgin olive oil, plus extra for greasing
2 tbsp pine nuts, to garnish (optional)
6 tbsp crème fraiche
2 tbsp lemon juice, plus extra if needed
2 tbsp tahini paste
fine sea salt

1 Preheat the oven to 200°C/Fan 180°C/Gas 6. Cut the aubergines in half lengthways, then make criss-cross cuts in the flesh at 2.5cm intervals with a small paring knife. Go as deep as you can, but be careful not to cut through to the skin.

2 Stuff the slices of garlic into the slits in the aubergines. Drizzle the aubergines with the olive oil and season with salt. Grease a baking sheet with a little oil and place the aubergines, cut side down, on the sheet, then roast for 30–40 minutes or until really soft.

3 Meanwhile, put the pine nuts, if using, in a small dry frying pan and toast them for a few minutes over a medium heat. Keep stirring them or shaking the pan so they don't burn. Set them aside.

4 Drain the cooked aubergines well on a wire rack – aubergines contain a lot of water so they must be drained before processing.

5 Place them (skin and all) in a blender or food processor. Add the crème fraîche, lemon juice and tahini, then blend until smooth. Season with salt and extra lemon juice if needed. Serve garnished with toasted pine nuts, if using.

ROASTED WHITE ONIONS

White onions are sweet and not too strong. I love their lovely caramelised flavour when roasted, and they make a perfect accompaniment to a roast dinner. This recipe is simple to do and utterly delicious.

SERVES 4

4 white onions
3 tbsp olive oil
2 garlic cloves, peeled
  and crushed
2 thyme sprigs
50g butter, diced
2 tbsp cider vinegar
1 tbsp demerara sugar
2 tbsp chopped parsley,
  to serve
flaked sea salt

1 Preheat the oven to 180°C/Fan 160°C/Gas 4. Trim off the tops of the onions and the 'hairy bit' from the root – do keep most of the root intact, though, so the onions don't fall apart. Peel the outer skin off the onions, then cut them into quarters through the root.

2 Place the onions in a single layer in a large baking tin. Don't pile them on top of each other or they will steam, not roast. Drizzle them with oil, then sprinkle with salt and toss well to coat. Add the garlic and thyme, put the tin in the preheated oven and roast the onions for 20–30 minutes.

3 Remove the tin from the oven and check that the onions have started to brown on top. If they haven't, put them back in the oven for another 5–10 minutes. Add the butter, vinegar and sugar to the tin, then gently turn the onions to coat them in the juices.

4 Put the onions back in the oven and cook them for a further 15–20 minutes or until they are golden brown and tender. Sprinkle them with chopped parsley and serve immediately.

VEGETABLES

SEARED SPRING GREENS WITH GARLIC, SMOKY BACON AND SUMAC

Spring greens and cabbage are quintessentially British vegetables, but I like pairing them with sumac, a citrusy Middle Eastern spice that's available in supermarkets nowadays. It gives a delightful little fizzing sensation on the tongue and goes beautifully with the greens and bacon.

SERVES 4

700g spring greens or green cabbage
60g butter
4 rashers of smoked streaky bacon, chopped
50g onion, peeled and finely chopped
2 garlic cloves, peeled and very finely chopped
2 tsp ground sumac
juice of ½ lemon
fine sea salt and black pepper

1 Remove the roots and any tough stems from the spring greens. If necessary, cut out the tough stalks from the centre of the leaves. Shred the leaves into pieces about 5mm wide. If using cabbage, trim it and shred the leaves.

2 Melt half the butter in a large frying pan over a gentle heat. Add the bacon and fry until brown, then add the onion and fry until soft. Add the greens and keep tossing them, as you would for a stir-fry but over a less fierce heat. Continue cooking the greens until soft, then add the garlic, sumac and the rest of the butter and cook for another couple of minutes.

3 Season with salt and pepper and lemon juice to taste.

BRAISED ASPARAGUS AND BROCCOLI WITH LEMON BUTTER

English asparagus has such a short season, so I like to use it as much as possible while it's at its best. It goes well with broccoli – and broccoli helps eke out the asparagus, which can be quite expensive.

SERVES 6

500g asparagus
2 tomatoes
2 tbsp olive oil
2 shallots, peeled
  and sliced
1 large head of broccoli,
  split into florets
60g butter
zest and juice of 2 lemons
flaked sea salt

1 Trim the asparagus and snap off the ends. If the skin on the stems looks a bit tough, peel the stems with a potato peeler.

2 Cut the tomatoes into quarters, cut out the seeds with a sharp knife and then cut each quarter into 2 strips.

3 Heat the olive oil in a frying pan over a medium heat. Add the shallots and brown them lightly, then add the broccoli florets and fry them for 1 minute. Add the asparagus and cook for 30 seconds, then stir in 3 tablespoons of water and cook until the water has evaporated.

4 Add the butter and lemon zest and juice, then stir them in well. Season with salt and garnish with the tomato strips.

BROCCOLI FLORETS AND STEMS

Broccoli is available all year round and is very nutritious. Many people throw the stems away, which is a shame, as they can be cooked separately and are good to eat. Choose a head of broccoli with a long, thick stem and trim off the rough end.

SERVES 4

1 head of broccoli
50g slivered or
    flaked almonds
30g butter
3 tbsp olive oil
3 garlic cloves, peeled
    and finely chopped
fine sea salt and
    black pepper

1   First prepare the broccoli. Remove the florets, leaving the stem in one piece.

2   Bring a pan of water to simmering point. Add the broccoli stem, simmer it for a moment, then drain it and refresh in cold water to stop the cooking process. Peel the stem and cut it into 4 pieces lengthwise, then set aside.

3   Toast the almonds in a dry, non-stick frying pan over a medium heat for a couple of minutes until golden brown.

4   Heat the butter and a tablespoon of oil in a pan. Add the broccoli florets, toasted almonds and garlic, then cook over a medium heat until the florets are just done. Set them aside to keep warm.

5   Wipe out the pan with kitchen paper and heat the remaining 2 tablespoons of oil. Add the pieces of stem and brown them all over, then season with salt and pepper.

6   Serve the stems and florets together.

HOME-MADE CRISPS

You won't believe how delicious these are. Yes, you do need a deep-fat fryer and a mandolin but if you have the right kit, crisps are not hard to make. I cook mine in two stages. The first stage, at 140°C, cooks the crisps without browning them too much. The second stage, at 180°C, browns them and makes them lovely and crunchy. If you were to put the crisps straight into the hotter oil, they would burn before they were cooked through.

SERVES 4

vegetable oil, for deep-frying
4 potatoes (Maris Pipers or Albert Bartlett Roosters work best), peeled
flaked sea salt

1 Heat the vegetable oil in a deep-fat fryer to 140°C. Getting the correct temperature is really important, so you do need to check with a cooking thermometer.

2 Slice the potatoes about 2–3mm thick on a mandolin. When the oil is hot, cook them in the fryer in small batches. Keep them moving with a slotted spoon so they don't stick together and cook for a couple of minutes until slightly soft and pliable. Remove each batch of crisps with a slotted spoon and place them on a baking tray.

3 Now heat the oil to 180°C. Again working in small batches, put the crisps in the hot oil and fry until golden brown and the oil has stopped bubbling. They will cook quickly at this heat, so be careful they don't get too brown.

4 Remove the crisps from the fryer and put them on kitchen paper or a cloth to drain. Immediately season with salt – the flakes will stick to the hot crisps.

5 Leave them to cool and then eat straight away or pack them into an airtight container and eat within 24 hours.

☕ COOK'S TIP ☕

I find that soaking the sliced potatoes in a bowl of cold water for 30 minutes, then drying them really well, helps make these crisps even crisper!

THE PERFECT ROAST POTATO

Who doesn't love roast potatoes? They are a simple dish but it's surprisingly tricky to get them just right – crispy on the outside and deliciously fluffy inside. The most important thing is to get the fat really hot to crisp up the outsides of the potatoes. Timing is crucial – they shouldn't be kept hanging about – so while your meat is resting is the ideal time for finishing the potatoes. Roast potatoes also need plenty of seasoning, so be generous and try sprinkling them with sesame or poppy seeds for a change.

SERVES 6 (DEPENDING ON GREED!)

150g goose fat
8 large floury potatoes
    (such as King
    Edwards or Albert
    Bartlett Roosters)
6 whole garlic cloves,
    unpeeled
4 thyme sprigs
4 rosemary sprigs
flaked sea salt

1 Preheat the oven to 240°C/Fan 220°C/Gas 9. Put the goose fat in a large roasting tin and place it in the oven while you peel the potatoes. The fat needs to be really hot.

2 Peel the potatoes and cut them into quarters, trying to make sure they are roughly the same size so they cook evenly. Put them in a large pan, cover with cold water and bring to the boil. Once the water is boiling, turn the heat down to a simmer and cook for 5–10 minutes – this will just start cooking the outside of the potatoes. Drain the potatoes well in a colander, then give them a good shake to fluff up the outsides – this helps them go crispy.

3 Once the potatoes are ready, carefully remove the roasting tin from the oven and place it on the hob over a medium heat. Lower the oven temperature to 220°C/Fan 200°C/Gas 7.

4 Gently lower the potatoes into the hot goose fat. The potatoes should sizzle as soon as they hit the fat. Then gently brown them in the hot fat until they are golden brown on all sides.

5 Add the garlic and herbs to the tin and put it back into the oven for 15–20 minutes. Then remove it from the oven and gently turn the potatoes over using a slotted spoon. (Be very careful with them at this stage, as you don't want to break them up.) Put the potatoes back in the oven and cook for another 15–20 minutes.

6 By this time the potatoes should be golden brown and crispy. If you feel they need a little more colour, gently turn them again and put them back into the oven for another 10 minutes or until the desired colour and texture is reached.

7 When the potatoes are done to your liking, remove them from the hot fat with a slotted spoon and put them on some kitchen paper or a cloth to remove any excess fat. Tip them into a warm dish and season with flaked sea salt – flakes are best as they stick to the hot potatoes. Serve at once.

GARLIC AND SESAME SEED POTATO WEDGES

These potato wedges are easier to prepare than roast potatoes and also absolutely delicious. The sesame seeds and garlic provide a gorgeous crunchy texture and loads of flavour. Great with the slow-roast lamb on page 190.

SERVES 6

1kg potatoes (Maris Pipers
   work well), peeled
4 tbsp rapeseed oil
3 garlic cloves, peeled
   and crushed
2 tsp flaked sea salt
1 tbsp white sesame seeds

1 Preheat the oven to 210°C/Fan 190°C/Gas 6½. Cut the potatoes into good-sized wedges and put them in a bowl. Mix the oil, garlic, salt and sesame seeds, then rub the mixture into the potatoes so they are nicely coated all over.

2 Tip the potatoes into a roasting tin and roast them for 45–50 minutes, turning them halfway through. Serve at once.

🥄 COOK'S TIP 🥄
You can also coat these little morsels with nigella seeds or even chopped chilli – great with barbecue food.

PATATAS BRAVAS

When this Spanish favourite is on a tapas menu, everyone orders it.
You just can't resist! Spicy and robust, this is great served as a part of
a tapas feast or as a side dish – or just on its own with a salad.

SERVES 6

3 tbsp olive oil
500g new potatoes,
    cut in half
4 garlic cloves, peeled,
    2 crushed and 2
    finely chopped
200g chorizo, sliced
1 white onion, peeled
    and diced
1 tsp sweet smoked
    paprika
2 rosemary sprigs,
    finely chopped
2 fresh red chillies
    (optional), seeded
    and finely chopped
1 tbsp tomato purée
400g can of tomatoes
1 tbsp balsamic vinegar,
    plus extra if needed
1 tsp golden caster sugar,
    plus extra if needed
chopped parsley, to serve
sea salt and cracked
    black pepper

1 Preheat the oven to 200°C/Fan 180°C/Gas 6. Add
2 tablespoons of the olive oil to a large roasting tin
and place it in the oven for 10 minutes to heat up.

2 Remove the tin from the oven and carefully place the
potatoes into the hot oil, then stir to coat them. Add
the crushed garlic and season generously with salt
and pepper. Roast the potatoes for 35–40 minutes,
turning them halfway through, until they are golden
brown and crisp.

3 Meanwhile, put a pan over a medium heat and add
the remaining tablespoon of olive oil and the sliced
chorizo. Sauté gently for 5 minutes until the chorizo
is crisp and its natural oils have been released. Add
the onion and the 2 cloves of finely chopped garlic to
the chorizo and continue to sauté over a gentle heat
for 5 minutes until the onions are soft and the garlic
is fragrant. Reduce the heat and stir in the smoked
paprika, rosemary, chillies, if using, and the tomato
purée and cook for 2 minutes. Keep the heat low so
you don't burn the paprika.

4 Roughly chop the tomatoes and add them to the pan
with the vinegar, caster sugar and a good pinch of
salt. Bring to the boil, then turn the heat down to a
gentle simmer and cook the sauce for 20–25 minutes
until it has thickened. Taste for seasoning and add
more vinegar if the sauce is too sweet or more sugar
if it tastes bitter.

5 When the potatoes and sauce are both ready, tip the
potatoes into an ovenproof serving dish, pour the
sauce over them and stir gently. Put the dish in the
oven for 10 minutes, then remove, sprinkle with
chopped parsley and serve immediately.

CELERIAC AND WHOLEGRAIN MUSTARD MASH

This is a lovely winter dish and a delicious change from ordinary mash.
The earthy celeriac flavour is perfect with game such as pheasant and partridge.

SERVES 6

1 celeriac, peeled
1 small floury
   potato, peeled
1 litre vegetable stock
2 tbsp double cream
50g butter
1 tbsp wholegrain
   mustard
2 tbsp finely chopped
   curly parsley
fine sea salt and
   white pepper

1 Cut the celeriac and the potato into 3cm dice. Put them in a pan with the stock and cook for 20 minutes until tender. Drain well.

2 Mash the celeriac and potato with a hand masher or put it all through a potato ricer, then add the cream and butter. Add the mustard and parsley, then season with salt and pepper to taste and serve at once. Alternatively, if you want a really smooth purée, mix it in a food processor.

3 You can make this in advance if you like, then tip it into a clean pan and reheat gently.

🥄 COOK'S TIP 🥄

If you would like a very white mash, cook the celeriac in a litre of whole milk instead of stock. You can then use the celeriac-flavoured milk in a soup.

CELERIAC REMOULADE

I like to serve this with smoked fish, such as mackerel, or even with gravadlax. It's so easy to prepare and is a great way of using celeriac.

SERVES 4

½ celeriac, peeled
juice of 1 lemon
6 tbsp mayonnaise
2 tsp drained capers,
   finely chopped
2 tsp finely chopped
   gherkins
1 anchovy fillet
   (from a can or jar),
   finely chopped
2 tsp Dijon mustard
1 tbsp finely chopped
   tarragon
1 tbsp finely chopped
   parsley
1 tsp golden caster sugar
½ tsp fine sea salt
white pepper

1 Cut the celeriac into fine matchsticks and put them in a bowl. Add some of the lemon juice to stop the celeriac going brown.

2 Add the remaining ingredients and taste for seasoning, then add more salt, pepper and lemon juice to taste. Leave for about 5 minutes before serving so the celeriac has time to soften.

RED ONION MARMALADE

This is the best thing to have in the fridge and it is utterly scrumptious.
Use it like chutney, add it to sandwiches or serve on the side with
cold meats and so on. It is easy to make and keeps well.

MAKES 1 MEDIUM JAR

3 red onions, peeled
100g golden caster sugar
50ml red wine vinegar
25ml balsamic vinegar
50ml red wine
50g redcurrant jelly

1 Slice the onions as finely as you can. A mandolin
slicer is ideal if you have one.

2 Put the sugar in a pan over a low heat and add
2 tablespoons of water. Let the sugar dissolve, then
turn up the heat and cook until the mixture turns
the colour of pale golden syrup. Be careful not to
let it go up the sides of the pan as this will ruin
the caramel and cause it to crystallise.

3 Pour the vinegars and the red wine into a separate
pan and add the redcurrant jelly. Bring to the boil,
then immediately add the contents of the pan to the
caramel and swish them around to bring everything
together. Add the onions to the pan, bring to a
simmer and then turn down the heat.

4 Cut a piece of greaseproof paper to fit the top of the
pan (the proper name for this is a cartouche) and
place it over the onions so it is touching them. Leave
the onions to cook over a low heat for 30–40 minutes,
stirring occasionally, until the mixture is reduced and
sticky. If the mixture gets too sticky, add a few drops
of water.

5 Tip the red onion marmalade into a sterilised jar
(see page 103), leave it to cool, then seal with a lid.
Store the jar in the fridge – this keeps for a couple
of months.

PEAS À LA FRANÇAISE

This is a simple and delicious way of serving peas and they look so pretty on the plate. It is important not to overcook the peas – you want them to stay nice and green – and to only add the lettuce at the last minute or it will go brown. This dish goes with everything and everyone loves it. I sometimes add a tiny pinch of chilli flakes to give it some extra oomph.

SERVES 6

1 tbsp olive oil
25g pancetta, diced
1 shallot, peeled and
  finely diced
1 garlic clove, peeled
  and sliced
100g chicken stock
250g frozen peas
25g butter
2 Little Gem lettuces,
  finely sliced
1 tbsp finely chopped
  parsley, to serve
fine sea salt

1 Heat the oil in a heavy-based pan and add the diced pancetta. Cook it over a high heat for 2–3 minutes or until the pancetta is golden brown and crisp.

2 Turn down the heat and add the shallot and garlic to the pan. Cook them gently over a low heat for 10 minutes until the shallot starts to brown.

3 Add the stock to the pan and bring it to a simmer, then add the peas and bring back to a simmer. Cook for 1 minute, then add the butter and cook for another minute before stirring in the lettuce. Season with salt to taste, sprinkle with parsley, then serve.

BALSAMIC-ROASTED BANANA SHALLOTS AND BEETROOT

This is an excellent winter warmer that celebrates the delicious sweetness of the ingredients. Scrunching bay leaves helps to bring out their flavour.

SERVES 4

250g banana shallots
300g baby beetroots, with
    tops, or large beetroot
    cut into 2cm cubes
3 tbsp aged balsamic
    vinegar
1 garlic bulb, cloves
    separated and peeled
3 tbsp olive oil
2 fresh bay leaves,
    scrunched
4 thyme sprigs (optional)
25g butter
flaked sea salt and
    black pepper

1 Preheat the oven to 200°C/Fan 180°C/Gas 6. Peel the shallots but leave the roots intact. No need to peel the baby beetroots at this stage. Put all the ingredients, except the butter, salt and pepper, into a roasting tin.

2 Cover the tin with foil and roast the shallots and beets in the preheated oven for 30–45 minutes, or until they are soft. Remove the foil and cook for another 15–20 minutes.

3 Take the tin out of the oven and, if using baby beets, allow them to cool a little before peeling off the skins. Put everything into a serving dish, add the butter, then mix and season well with salt and pepper. (See image, opposite.)

BEER-PICKLED SHALLOT RINGS

These are perfect for serving with cheese or cold beef and they're also nice for adding a bit of crunch and flavour to a sandwich.

MAKES 1 JAR

10 banana shallots
250ml good local ale,
    such as Old Peculier
150ml white wine vinegar
150g muscovado sugar
1 tsp maple syrup
6 thyme sprigs
2 garlic cloves, peeled
    and crushed
1 star anise

1 Start by peeling the banana shallots. Cut the tops off but leave the roots intact to help keep the shallot together when you are slicing it. Slice the shallots into rings about 5mm thick, then place them in a 1-litre sterilised jar (see page 103).

2 Put all the other ingredients in a pan and bring them to the boil. Pour the hot liquid over the shallot rings and seal the jar with a lid. Store for up to 3 weeks in the fridge before using to allow time for the flavours to develop.

PICKLED BEETROOT WITH CIDER VINEGAR

Simple to make and very tasty, this pickled beetroot is good with cold meats and pâté or to add flavour to salads or red cabbage. Beetroot goes well with smoked fish, so you could dice some to add as a garnish.

MAKES 2–3 JARS

800g raw beetroots,
  with skin and roots
2 garlic bulbs, cloves
  separated and peeled
2 tbsp olive oil
flaked sea salt

Pickling mix
700ml cider vinegar
125g dark soft
  brown sugar
3 fresh bay leaves
1 tbsp whole black
  peppercorns
1 tbsp allspice berries
1 fresh red chilli, chopped
1 tsp fine sea salt

1 Preheat the oven to 200°C/Fan 180°C/Gas 6. Put the beetroot and garlic in a roasting tin, drizzle over the olive oil and season with salt, then cover the tin with foil. Bake the beetroot for 1½ hours or until tender, but remove the garlic after 15–20 minutes and set it aside, as you don't want it to be too soft.

2 When the beets are cooked, set them aside until they are cool enough to handle, then peel them. Wear rubber gloves if you're worried about staining your hands. Cut the beetroot into 1cm dice and put them with the garlic into 2 or 3 sterilised jars.

3 To make the pickling mix, put the vinegar and all the other ingredients in a pan. Slowly bring it to the boil, then simmer for 5 minutes. Pour the mixture over the beetroots and garlic, then seal the tops of the jars with the lids immediately.

4 Ideally, leave the beetroot for a couple of weeks before using. It will keep for ages, but once opened store it in the fridge.

🍴 COOK'S TIP 🍴
To sterilise jars, wash and dry them well, then put them in a low oven (140°C/Fan 120°C/Gas 1) for 10–15 minutes. If using Kilner jars, remove the rubber seals before putting the jars in the oven.

BOULANGÈRE AND DAUPHINOISE POTATOES

These recipes are classic French treats and incredibly tasty. I love them both but the boulangère is less rich than the creamy dauphinoise and you can make it with vegetable stock instead of chicken for a vegetarian dish.

SERVES 4

Boulangère
200g butter, plus extra
   for greasing
1 tbsp oil
3 large white onions,
   peeled and finely sliced
4 thyme sprigs, leaves
   only, finely chopped
1kg floury potatoes (such
   as Maris Pipers), peeled
500ml chicken stock
flaked sea salt and
   black pepper

Dauphinoise
250ml whole milk
250ml double cream
2 garlic cloves
2 thyme sprigs
100g butter, plus extra
   for greasing
1kg floury potatoes (such
   as Maris Pipers), peeled
flaked sea salt and
   white pepper

Boulangère potatoes

1 First prepare the caramelised onions. Place a large pan over a medium heat and add 100g of the butter and the oil. Add the sliced onions, thyme and a good pinch of salt. Cook the onions over a gentle heat for 15–20 minutes or until they are dark brown in colour. Don't stir the onions too often, as this will break contact with the pan and cause the process to take twice as long. Once the onions are a good colour, season them with salt and pepper to taste, remove from the pan and set aside.

2 Preheat the oven to 180°C/Fan 160°C/Gas 4. Butter an ovenproof dish, then melt the remaining butter in a small pan. Finely slice the potatoes using a mandolin if you have one, as this keeps the slices a nice even thickness. Put the potato slices in a large bowl, pour the melted butter over them and then season with salt and pepper.

3 Add 2 layers of potato slices to the buttered dish, making sure each slice is overlapping the next. Next add a layer of caramelised onions, then another 2 layers of potato and another layer of onions. Repeat this process until the dish is full, finishing with a layer of potatoes.

4 Warm the stock and season it well, then pour it over the potatoes to just cover. Cover the dish with a piece of greaseproof paper – it should touch the top of the potatoes. Bake in the preheated oven for 45 minutes or until a small sharp knife can be inserted into the centre easily with no resistance. Remove the paper and bake for another 10 minutes until the top is golden brown. Serve at once from the dish.

Dauphinoise potatoes

1 Put the milk and cream in a pan with the garlic and thyme. Season generously with salt and bring to the boil, then remove the pan from the heat and set aside.

2 Preheat the oven to 180°C/Fan 160°C/Gas 4. Butter a gratin dish well. Finely slice the potatoes and layer them in the dish, overlapping them as for the boulangère, and pressing them down. Pour the milk and cream mixture over the top and dot with butter.

3 Cover with a piece of buttered greaseproof paper and bake for 1 hour or until a small sharp knife can be inserted into the centre with no resistance. Remove the paper and bake for another 10 minutes until the top is golden brown. Serve at once from the dish.

🍴 COOK'S TIP 🍴

If you want to get ahead with the dauphinoise, line the buttered dish with greaseproof paper and proceed as above. When the dish is cooked, leave it to get cold. When you're ready to serve, turn it out on to a board and cut into squares. Then reheat the squares in a preheated oven (200°C/Fan 180°C/Gas 6) for about 15 minutes.

PEACH AND BLUE CHEESE TARTE TATIN

I think peaches and blue cheese are a marriage made in heaven and they work brilliantly in this tarte tatin. You can make it in a special tatin tin or in an ovenproof frying pan. I like to include the balsamic reduction to drizzle over before serving to add extra flavour. This recipe makes more of the balsamic mixture than you need, but just pour it into a bottle and save it for a salad.

SERVES 4

1 x 375g packet of
　puff pastry
plain flour, for dusting
60g golden caster sugar
30ml white wine vinegar
50g butter
2 rosemary sprigs, finely
　chopped
4 peaches, cut in half
　and stoned
60g blue cheese, crumbled
rocket leaves, to garnish

Balsamic reduction
200ml balsamic vinegar
150g golden caster sugar
1 garlic clove, peeled
　and crushed
1 thyme sprig
2 thin strips of orange
　peel

1　First make the balsamic reduction. Place all the ingredients in a pan, bring to the boil and reduce to the consistency of a light syrup. Set it aside for later.

2　On a lightly floured work surface, roll out the puff pastry into a circle a few centimetres bigger than the pan you are going to use. Prick it with a fork, then chill it in the fridge until needed. Preheat the oven to 200°C/Fan 180°C/Gas 6.

3　Put the sugar in a frying pan with 3 tablespoons of water and cook until a caramel is formed. Heat the vinegar, then add it to the pan with the butter and swirl them around to amalgamate. Add the rosemary. Pour the mixture into your tatin pan, if using, or leave it in the frying pan.

4　Place the peaches, cut side down, on the caramel. Top with the puff pastry, tucking the pastry in around the peaches.

5　Bake in the preheated oven for about 30 minutes or until the pastry is golden brown and cooked throughout. Remove and invert on to a baking tray right away. Sprinkle the blue cheese on top, then place back in the oven for 3 minutes or until the blue cheese has melted. Finish with rocket leaves and drizzle about a tablespoon of the balsamic reduction over the top.

PULSES & GRAINS

*The chapter begins with the basics, then progresses, skill by skill,
recipe by recipe, up to showpiece dishes that really wow.*

NO KITCHEN STORE CUPBOARD IS COMPLETE without a selection of pulses and grains. Beans, lentils, rice and other grains, such as couscous, are staple foods the world over. They are nutritious, filling and generally not expensive and they can be both the centre of a meal or an accompaniment. I love them all and in the following pages you'll find recipes for a variety of dishes from perfect basic rice to fabulous bean dishes and risottos. When I worked as a chef in the Hebrides, I relied on pulses and grains for making a good variety of dishes when there was a shortage of fresh vegetables.

PULSES

I am never without a good selection of pulses – different kinds of dried beans and lentils as well as chickpeas. They are great for adding to stews, curries and soups, making dips and for bulking up salads. They keep well, though I do try not to exceed their use-by date, as old beans take longer to cook and may not taste as good. Store pulses in airtight containers in a cool, dark, dry cupboard.

Pulses are actually the edible seeds of certain plants. They contain carbohydrate, but as they are also rich in protein and fibre, a good source of B vitamins and minerals and contain little or no fat, they are a very healthy food. I think they are great when you are trying to lose weight, as they feel substantial but are actually not that calorific. Butter beans are one of my favourites and a 100-gram serving contains only about 100 calories.

SOAKING AND COOKING PULSES

Dried beans do need soaking in cold water overnight if possible to partially rehydrate them. Soaking pulses can be an issue for some people, but it really is no trouble – as long as you remember the night before

you plan to use them. Once soaked, the beans cook more quickly and it is said that they are easier to digest. However, if you forget to soak your beans overnight, you can put them to soak in just-boiled water for as long as you can.

Most lentils don't need soaking, but mung beans do benefit from soaking for about four hours. They then cook quickly.

When cooking beans and lentils, don't add salt, as this stops them becoming properly tender. Season them once they are cooked. When cooking soaked beans, put them in cold water, bring to the boil and let any froth come to the surface. Drain the beans and rinse them under cold water, then put them in a pan of fresh water. With kidney beans and soya beans be sure to boil them rapidly for 10 minutes before reducing the heat for the rest of the cooking time. This helps to destroy any toxins in the beans.

🍴 COOK'S TIP 🍴

When making houmous, try adding a few ice cubes with the chickpeas. This helps to make lovely soft purée.

When cooking chickpeas and black beans, add a teaspoon of bicarbonate of soda to the water – this helps to soften them.

Canned beans and chickpeas are fine for most dishes but don't have quite as much texture and flavour as the dried varieties. I do suggest that you drain and rinse them before using. You can also buy ready-cooked lentils in packets but these are far more expensive than cooking your own.

You can keep cooked beans and lentils in the fridge for a few days and they also freeze well.

RICE

Choose your rice carefully and buy the best you can afford. With rice, you do get what you pay for and you can taste the difference in a good-quality rice. There are thousands of different kinds and it is important to use the correct type for your dish – there's no point trying to make a risotto with basmati rice, for instance.

For risottos, choose Italian Carnaroli or Arborio rice. For paella, look for short-grain Spanish rice. For pilaus, I like basmati, while for salads I sometimes use wild black rice.

Basmati is probably the rice I use most often and the best kind comes from the region around the Himalayas. There are so many ways of cooking it and everyone swears by their technique but I prefer the absorption method as described on page 112. It's quick, easy and you don't need to drain the rice.

It's also really nice to add extra flavour to your rice. For example, you can sauté some thin slices of onion in oil, then add the rice and a few saffron threads that you have soaked in a tablespoon of boiling water. Stir, then cook the rice as usual. You can add cumin or chilli in the same way or stir some fresh herbs through the rice once it is cooked.

Raw rice does need to be stored in an airtight container. It keeps well but it can get mouldy so do check use-by dates.

You do need to be careful about using leftover rice. Raw rice may contain bacteria that can survive when the rice is cooked. If the rice is then left standing around at room temperature, the bacteria can multiply and cause food poisoning. The main thing to remember is to cool any leftover rice as quickly as possible and store it in the fridge in a covered container. Don't leave it lying around in a warm kitchen. I often use leftover rice cold in a salad the next day, or you can reheat it thoroughly as part of a stir-fry. Don't keep cooked rice any longer than a day.

OTHER GRAINS

- **Couscous** is made of steamed balls of wheat and is quick to cook and delicious with stews, tagines and in salads. I'm particularly fond of jumbo couscous as I love the texture. You can dress couscous up with all sorts of flavours – spices, such as turmeric, ginger, cumin, star anise or cinnamon, or with herbs, such as coriander and parsley. It's good hot or cold.
- **Pearl barley** is another great favourite of mine and very nutritious. It's lovely in soup and also makes an excellent risotto. When using barley for risotto, you can add the liquid all at once – no standing around stirring – so it's very easy!
- **Quinoa** is actually a seed not a grain. It is high in nutrients and – unlike rice – is a complete protein. Ideal for people who are gluten- or wheat-intolerant, quinoa is great in salads or as accompaniment. See page 59 for a great quinoa recipe.
- **Bulgur wheat** is made from wheat grains that have been cracked and partially cooked. It's high in fibre and low in fat, so a good healthy food. See page 60 for a salad recipe using bulgur.

111

PERFECT RICE

Lots of people are worried about cooking rice but it is easy, as long as you wash it well to remove excess starch, then follow this simple method. You can safely keep any rice until the next day to use in a stir-fry, but make sure you heat it through over a high heat. Or you can serve it cold in a salad. Store cooked rice in the fridge and don't keep it any longer than a day.

SERVES 4

300g long-grain
   basmati rice
2 tsp flaked sea salt
25g unsalted butter

1 First wash the rice under cold running water for about 5 minutes or until the water runs clear. Alternatively, put it in a bowl of cold water, stir well, then drain and rinse the rice under cold water.

2 Put the rice in a medium-sized pan and add 550ml of water and a teaspoon of the salt. Don't stir too much or more starch will be released. Bring the water to a simmer, put a tight-fitting lid on the pan and leave it over a low heat for 10 minutes.

3 Take the pan off the heat, but do not remove the lid, and leave the rice to stand for another 15 minutes. Take the lid off the pan, fluff up the rice with a fork and mix in the remaining salt and the butter.

PILAU RICE

SERVES 4

350g basmati rice
50g butter
1 tsp ground cinnamon
   or ½ cinnamon stick
seeds from 6 cardamom
   pods, crushed
1 scant tsp ground
   turmeric
2 tsp flaked sea salt

1 Wash the rice under cold running water for 5 minutes to remove any excess starch.

2 Put the rice, butter, spices and one teaspoon of the salt in a large pan with 500ml of water. Place over a medium heat until the water is boiling and the butter has melted.

3 Stir the rice, then cover the pan and leave to simmer for 10 minutes. Take the pan off the heat, but don't remove the lid, and leave the rice to stand for 15 minutes. Fluff up the rice with a fork, mix in the rest of the salt and tip the rice into a warm bowl to serve.

GREEN HERB COUSCOUS

Couscous is a staple of North African cuisine and has become hugely
popular in the UK too. I love it. It's made from steamed balls of
crushed durum wheat, so is really like a kind of pasta. Serve this
beautiful green dish as a salad for lunch or as an accompaniment
to lamb or other meat dishes – it's great for soaking up juices.

SERVES 4–6

200g couscous (regular,
  not jumbo)
250ml just-boiled water
4 tbsp olive oil
2 banana shallots, peeled
  and finely diced
1 garlic clove, peeled
  and finely chopped
bunch of flatleaf parsley
bunch of chervil
bunch of chives
bunch of tarragon
1 tsp runny honey
juice of 1 lemon
fine sea salt and cracked
  black pepper

1 Place the couscous in a heatproof container, add
  the water, cover and leave for 5 minutes. The heat
  from the water will be enough to cook the couscous.

2 Meanwhile, heat the olive oil in a pan, add the
  shallots and garlic and cook over a medium heat
  for 2–3 minutes or until softened but not coloured.
  Set aside.

3 Pick all the leaves off the herb stalks – use the stalks
  in another dish, such as soup. Place the leaves in
  a blender and blitz until finely chopped, or finely
  chop them with a knife. This helps to release the
  chlorophyll, which will give the couscous a lovely
  bright green colour.

4 Tip the couscous into a large mixing bowl, break it up
  with a fork and mix in the cooked shallots, garlic and
  their oil, the honey and the chopped herbs. Finish
  with lemon juice, salt and pepper to taste.

CUMIN AND LIME SPICED LENTILS

These spicy lentils go beautifully with chicken and lamb dishes or you can eat them on their own with salad. Yes, there is quite a lot of cumin but you do need it here and it works well. It's worth making plenty, as the lentils keep well in the fridge for several days.

SERVES 4–6

2 tbsp vegetable oil
70g butter
1 medium carrot, peeled
   and finely diced
1 leek, washed and
   finely diced
1 celery stick, finely diced
2 banana shallots, peeled
   and finely diced
4 garlic cloves, peeled
   and finely chopped
1 tbsp ground cumin
200g Puy lentils
juice and zest of 2 limes
700ml vegetable stock
pinch of saffron strands
4 tbsp roughly chopped
   coriander
fine sea salt and
   black pepper

1 Place a large pan over a medium heat and add the oil and butter. Once the butter has melted, add the carrot, leek, celery, shallots and garlic and cook them for 5 minutes until soft and just starting to brown.

2 Turn the heat down to low and add the ground cumin. Stir it through the vegetables for 5 minutes but make sure it doesn't burn – cooking spices like this helps to release their full flavour.

3 Rinse the lentils and add them to the pan with the lime juice, vegetable stock and saffron. Bring to the boil, then turn the heat down to a simmer and cook for 20–25 minutes until the lentils have absorbed all the liquid and are soft.

4 Season to taste with salt and pepper, then stir in the lime zest and chopped coriander just before serving.

115

PULSES &
GRAINS

HARISSA HOUMOUS

This houmous has lots of extra flavour from the harissa and it's good served with pitta bread or sticks of raw vegetables as a snack or starter. Making your own harissa paste is so simple and it tastes really delicious. The recipe here makes more than enough for the houmous, so keep the rest in a jar in the fridge and use it with chicken or other meat or add a teaspoon to salad dressing to give a boost of wonderful flavour. Using roasted red peppers from a jar and bought sundried tomatoes is fine here and makes life much easier.

SERVES 4

400g can of chickpeas, drained
juice and zest of 1 lemon
1 garlic clove, peeled and crushed
1 tsp ground cumin
100ml tahini
4 tbsp extra virgin olive oil, plus extra to pour on top of the houmous
fine sea salt

Harissa paste
1 tsp cumin seeds
1 tsp fennel seeds
2 tsp coriander seeds
1 tsp caraway seeds
2 tsp dried chilli flakes
5 tbsp olive oil
5 garlic cloves, peeled
1 tbsp sweet smoked paprika
2 roasted red peppers (from a jar)
400g sundried tomatoes in oil
2 fresh red chillies or 1 fresh bird's eye chilli
bunch of coriander, roughly chopped

1 Start by making the harissa paste. Place a small pan over a low heat and add the cumin, fennel, coriander and caraway seeds and the chilli flakes. Gently toast them for 3–4 minutes until fragrant to bring out their flavour. Remove the pan from the heat and leave the spices to cool slightly, then grind them in a spice grinder or with a pestle and mortar to form a fine powder. Set this spice mix aside.

2 Place the pan back over the heat and add the olive oil. When the oil is warm, stir in the garlic and smoked paprika. Gently cook over a gentle heat for 2–3 minutes, taking care not to burn the paprika (burnt spices taste very bitter).

3 Strain and pat dry the peppers and the sundried tomatoes, then add them to the pan, along with the fresh chillies and coriander. Cook over a low heat for a further 2 minutes, then put everything into a food processor and add the spice mix. Blitz for 2–3 minutes until smooth, then transfer the paste to an airtight container. You can use it as a marinade and in other sauces as well as for this dish.

4 For the houmous, rinse the chickpeas in cold water to remove any excess starch. Put them in a food processor with the lemon juice and zest, garlic, cumin, tahini and olive oil, then add a tablespoon of the harissa paste. Blend to a purée, then add more harissa to taste and season with salt. Transfer the houmous to a bowl or individual ramekins and drizzle it with olive oil to stop it discolouring.

REFRIED BEANS

This is an essential part of the famous Mexican breakfast dish known as 'huevos rancheros', but I also like to serve it with chicken, barbecue food or anything I fancy. Great with spicy chilli sausages! It's really substantial and delicious.

SERVES 4

200g dried pinto
    or black beans,
    soaked overnight
2 oregano sprigs
2 tbsp vegetable oil
6 rashers of smoked
    streaky bacon, cut
    into small strips
50g butter
2 banana shallots, peeled
    and finely chopped
4 garlic cloves, peeled
    and finely chopped
1 tbsp ground cumin
1 tsp chilli powder
    (optional)
2 tbsp roughly chopped
    coriander, to garnish
4 lime wedges, to garnish
fine sea salt

1 Drain the beans and put them in a large pan with the oregano. Cover generously with cold water. Bring to the boil, then turn the heat down to a simmer and cook the beans gently for 1½–2 hours or until soft. Keep an eye on the beans to make sure they don't dry out – add more just-boiled water if necessary.

2 When the beans are done, drain them in a colander, reserving the liquid. Set both the beans and cooking liquid to one side. Discard the oregano.

3 Heat the oil in a large heavy-based pan and cook the bacon over a medium heat until golden brown and crisp. Add the butter, shallots and garlic to the pan and cook for 5 minutes until the shallots start to brown. Then add the cumin and chilli powder, if using, and cook for 1 minute.

4 Pour the beans and a splash of the cooking liquid into the pan. Using a potato masher, break the beans down to make a rough purée as they warm through. If the purée seems too thick, add a little more of the cooking liquid. Season with salt to taste.

5 Put the refried beans into ramekins or into a large bowl and serve garnished with the chopped coriander and lime wedges.

MUNG BEAN, GINGER, SWEETCORN AND SPINACH SOUP

This is a wonderfully tasty, hearty and healthy soup – and it is extremely filling, so great when you are on a diet. It's good to make this in advance if you can, then leave it for a few hours for the flavours to develop before finishing with the spinach. Don't forget to soak the mung beans first.

SERVES 4–6

150g yellow split mung
　　beans or yellow lentils,
　　soaked for 3–4 hours
1.5 litres vegetable stock
15g fresh root ginger,
　　peeled and cut into
　　matchsticks, reserving
　　the peel from the ginger
1 heaped tsp ground
　　turmeric
1 tbsp coconut or olive oil
1 white onion, peeled
　　and finely chopped
1 red chilli, finely chopped
1 fennel bulb, trimmed
　　and finely chopped
340g can of sweetcorn,
　　drained and rinsed
250g baby spinach,
　　washed
fine sea salt and
　　black pepper

1　Drain the mung beans or lentils, put them in a large pan of cold water and bring to the boil. Turn the heat down to a simmer and cook for 1 minute. Drain, then rinse the beans well under cold water to remove all the scum.

2　Rinse out the pan and add the cooked mung beans or lentils with the stock. Add the ginger peel and the turmeric, bring to the boil, then turn the heat down and simmer for 20–30 minutes or until the beans or lentils have softened. The exact timing will depend on the pulses you are using, but mung beans do soften quickly, so keep an eye on them and don't let them go mushy.

3　Meanwhile, heat the coconut oil in a large frying pan. Add the onion and cook until softened, then add the chilli, fennel and sliced root ginger and continue to cook gently until softened. Add the sweetcorn and cook for 1 more minute.

4　Add this mixture to the cooked mung beans or lentils and season well with salt and pepper, then set aside.

5　When you are ready to serve, bring the soup up to a simmer, then turn off the heat and throw in the spinach so it just wilts slightly rather than cooks. Remove the ginger peel and serve the soup at once in deep bowls.

HOME-MADE BAKED BEANS WITH SMOKED PAPRIKA

There's nothing like home-made baked beans. They are so satisfying to make, really inexpensive and incredibly delicious. They're good for you, too, and contain less sugar than the canned versions.

SERVES 6

250g dried haricot beans, soaked overnight
1 carrot, peeled and cut into large wedges
1 onion, peeled and cut into large wedges
1 celery stick, cut into large chunks
1 bay leaf
parsley stalks
fine sea salt

Sauce
1 tbsp olive oil
300g onions, peeled and finely chopped
4 garlic cloves, peeled and finely chopped
1 fresh red chilli, chopped (optional)
4 tbsp tomato ketchup
2 tbsp tomato purée
1 tbsp sweet smoked paprika
250g canned tomatoes, chopped
2 tbsp golden caster sugar
1 tbsp Worcestershire sauce
splash of Tabasco sauce

1 Drain the beans, put them in a large pan and add cold water to cover. Add the carrot, onion, celery, bay leaf and parsley stalks. Bring to the boil, then turn the heat down and simmer for about an hour and 10 minutes or until the beans are tender. Add more water if the liquid reduces too much.

2 Once the beans are cooked, strain them, reserving the cooking water. Discard the carrot, onion, celery, bay leaf and parsley stalks.

3 Meanwhile, make the sauce. Heat the oil in a large non-stick frying pan, add the onions, garlic and chilli and cook for 2 minutes over a low heat. Now add the remaining ingredients and 600ml of the reserved cooking water – if you don't have enough, top it up with water. Cook gently for a further 10 minutes. Remove the pan and blend the mixture until smooth in a food processor or blender. Preheat the oven to 200°C/Fan 180°C/Gas 6.

4 Tip the cooked beans and the tomato sauce into a large casserole dish and add a pinch of salt. Cover the dish, place it in the preheated oven and cook for 20 minutes, then turn the heat down to 170°C/Fan 150°C/Gas 3½ and cook for another hour and 10 minutes. Serve at once or cool and store in the fridge. These beans keep well for a few days.

MERGUEZ, CHORIZO AND BUTTER BEAN CASSOULET

This is a proper winter warmer, packed with spicy sausages and great flavours.
You may like to cook your beans from dried if you have time, but I often use
canned for speed and ease. I'm all for making life easy when possible.

SERVES 4–6

2 tbsp olive oil
500g merguez (spicy
  North African sausages)
80g smoked bacon
  or pancetta, cut
  into small strips
140g chorizo, sliced
1 white onion, peeled
  and finely chopped
2 garlic cloves, crushed
½ tsp sweet smoked
  paprika
100ml good-quality
  red wine
400g can of tomatoes,
  drained
400g can of butter
  beans, drained
250ml chicken stock
1 tbsp chopped tarragon

1 Preheat the oven to 180°C/Fan 160°C/Gas 4. Place a
  flameproof casserole dish over a medium heat and
  add a tablespoon of the oil. Add the merguez and
  cook them on all sides until golden brown. Remove
  them from the pan and set aside.

2 Add the remaining tablespoon of oil and then the
  smoked bacon or pancetta and the chorizo. Cook over
  a medium heat until they have both browned and
  the chorizo has released its oils. Add the onion and
  garlic and sauté for 3–4 minutes until the onion has
  softened. Stir in the smoked paprika and cook for a
  couple of minutes to release the maximum flavour.

3 Add the wine, bring to the boil and cook until it has
  reduced by half. Now add the tomatoes, butter beans,
  browned merguez and the chicken stock and bring
  back to the boil. Cover the dish and place it in the
  preheated oven for 40 minutes or until the sauce
  has nicely reduced.

4 Remove the casserole dish from the oven and add
  the chopped tarragon. This is meant to be quite an
  oily dish but you can drain off some of the chorizo
  oil if you like. Serve immediately with some hunks
  of good crusty bread.

CHANA DAL

I love dal and I know that every household in India cooks dal differently.
This excellent recipe comes from my friend Romy Gill, who is the queen of
Indian cooking and teaches an amazing course at my cookery school.

SERVES 4–6

250g chana dal
  (yellow split peas)
500ml just-boiled water
1 tsp ground turmeric
4 tsp rapeseed oil
1 tsp nigella seeds
1 medium red onion,
  peeled and finely
  chopped
2 garlic cloves, peeled
  and chopped
20g fresh root ginger,
  peeled and grated
1 tsp ground cumin or
  crushed whole seeds
1 tsp ground coriander or
  crushed whole seeds
2 fresh green chillies,
  chopped
1 large tomato,
  finely chopped
2 tsp chopped fresh
  coriander
fine sea salt

1 Soak the chana dal in cold water for 15–20 minutes, then wash it in cold water to remove the starch.

2 Put the dal in a deep pan with the just-boiled water, add the turmeric and half a teaspoon of salt, then cook for 30 minutes over a medium heat.

3 Heat the oil in a separate pan, add the nigella seeds and allow them to pop. Add the chopped onion and cook it gently and slowly until softened, but don't allow it to brown. Add the garlic and ginger and cook for another 6–7 minutes over a medium heat. Add the cumin and coriander to the paste, then the chillies and tomato, and cook for another 2–3 minutes. Keep stirring so that the paste doesn't burn. If the paste does start to stick to the pan, add a few drops of hot water.

4 Add the cooked dal to the paste and mix well. Cover the pan and cook the dal over a very low heat for 2–3 minutes. Season with salt to taste, add the fresh coriander, then serve.

PULSES &
GRAINS

PEARL BARLEY RISOTTO

This British version of risotto has become so popular and I'm glad, as I think barley is such a delicious and nutritious grain. Do make sure you wash it well, though. You don't have to soak pearl barley, but soaking does remove excess starch and reduces the cooking time.

SERVES 4

50g butter
2 banana shallots, peeled and finely diced
1 medium carrot, peeled and finely diced
1 leek, washed and finely diced
200g pearl barley, soaked for 2 hours, then rinsed
600ml hot chicken stock, plus extra if needed
100ml double cream
juice of 1 lemon
100g Parmesan cheese, grated
6 tbsp chopped parsley
2 tbsp chopped chervil
fine sea salt and white pepper

1 Melt the butter in a heavy-based pan and add the diced vegetables. Cook them gently over a low heat for about 10 minutes, or until soft and fragrant, without allowing them to brown.

2 Add the soaked, drained pearl barley and stir well. Add half the stock and stir, then bring to a simmer and cook for about 10 minutes before adding the rest of the stock. Continue to cook until all the stock has been absorbed. If the barley is not quite done, add a little more stock or water and cook until the barley is tender.

3 Next add the double cream, bring to a simmer and cook for another few minutes. Season well with salt and pepper, then stir in the lemon juice and Parmesan. Finish with the fresh herbs and serve right away.

PEA, FETA AND BROWN BUTTER RISOTTO

Chefs love brown butter for its rich nutty flavour – the posh name is 'beurre noisette'. It's not hard to make but you do need to get it just right so you have the taste without burning the butter. Take your time and you'll be fine. It really does add a nice touch to this risotto.

SERVES 4

100g butter
50ml good-quality olive oil
2 banana shallots, peeled
    and finely chopped
1 garlic clove, peeled
    and finely chopped
200g Arborio rice
100ml dry white wine
1 litre vegetable stock
200g peas (fresh
    or frozen)
75g Parmesan
    cheese, grated
juice of 1 lemon
2 tbsp finely sliced
    mint leaves
2 tbsp roughly
    chopped parsley
100g feta cheese,
    crumbled
handful of rocket leaves
flaked sea salt and
    black pepper

1 Place a heavy-based pan over a gentle heat and add the butter. Heat the butter until the milk solids (the white scum) separate and the butter starts to brown, then take the pan off the heat before the butter burns. Pour the brown butter into a bowl and set it aside.

2 Add the olive oil, shallots and garlic to the pan. Cook them over a low heat for 5–6 minutes until softened. Turn up the heat and add the rice, stirring to coat it in the oil. Pour in the wine and simmer, while stirring constantly, until the liquid has evaporated. Meanwhile, warm the stock in a separate pan and keep it at simmering point.

3 Add the hot stock to the rice, one ladle at a time, reserving a ladleful to finish the risotto. Keep stirring and cook for about 25 minutes until all the liquid has been absorbed and the rice is tender.

4 Stir the reserved stock into the risotto and add the peas. Cook for 2 minutes for fresh peas or 4 minutes for frozen. Add most of the brown butter and all the Parmesan and stir vigorously. This will help the risotto become creamy.

5 Finish with the lemon juice, fresh herbs, feta cheese and most of the rocket. Season with salt and pepper to taste, drizzle with the remaining brown butter and serve at once, garnished with the rest of the rocket.

FISH & SHELLFISH

The chapter begins with the basics, then progresses, skill by skill, recipe by recipe, up to showpiece dishes that really wow.

LIVING AND WORKING IN THE HEBRIDES was such a great experience for a chef like me, as there was an abundance of the most wonderful fish and shellfish. We had beautiful halibut, turbot, squid, lobsters, langoustine, crabs, scallops – everything you could want. Now I live in the southeast of England, but I still cook a great deal of fish and shellfish. In this chapter I want to guide you through a number of dishes, from a crab salad and simple seared salmon to crispy battered cod and curried scallops.

My own seafood favourites are probably turbot and crab – I adore the wonderful flavour of crab. I know many people are nervous of cooking fish and shellfish, but let me assure you that there's nothing difficult about it once you get to know the basics. Most fish dishes are quick to cook and I find that the less you fiddle about with fish the better. I do like to cook fish on the bone for the best flavour, but fillets are more suitable for some dishes and they're so easy to cook.

Fishmongers should be happy to fillet and scale fish for you. If you do want to try filleting for yourself, get yourself a flexible filleting knife. It makes things a lot easier.

BUYING AND STORING FISH
Seafood deteriorates much more quickly than most types of meat. Don't buy anything that's more than one day or at most a couple of days old. Avoid fish or seafood that has been on display for extended periods, even if it's on ice. If there isn't any fresh fish or seafood available, fish or seafood that has been frozen at sea is your next best bet. This is what to look out for.
- Fresh fish should be firm and the flesh should spring back when touched.
- When buying whole fish, check that the eyes are bright, clear and not sunken, and the gills are dark red – the paler they are, the older the fish. If you want fillets, ask the fishmonger to fillet the fish for you – and take the bones so you can make your own stock. You'll find a recipe on page 274. It's not difficult and it's so worthwhile.
- Smell the fish – there should be no strong odours. If it has a strong 'fishy' smell, it is not fresh and not for you. Ask at the counter when the fish came in. Shellfish, such as prawns, should also smell fresh and should look moist and plump – not dry or cracked.
- If you are shopping at a supermarket, buy fresh fish or seafood when you've done the rest of your shopping, take it straight home, and cook it within 24 hours.
- Keep fish as cold as possible until you are ready to cook it. Store it in the coldest part of your refrigerator. When you're ready to cook the fish, rinse it with cold water.

SUSTAINABILITY
We're all aware now of the problems caused by overfishing and damaging fishing methods, so do your best to buy fish that comes from sustainable sources. The Marine Stewardship Council is an

organisation set up to protect the world's oceans and safeguard seafood supplies. Fish and other seafood certified by the MSC come from sustainable sources, so look for their label or talk to your fishmonger to find out more about the fish you're thinking of buying.

Fish farming is widespread now, particularly of some types such as sea bass and salmon. The flavour and texture of farmed fish is slightly different but it is generally fine, though not as good as wild. The price of fish such as wild salmon is prohibitive nowadays, but it is worth having once in a while for a special treat.

TYPES OF FISH

There are two main groups – white fish and oily fish. White fish store their fat reserves in the liver, while oily fish store fat in their flesh as well as in the liver. All fish is an excellent source of protein and white fish is relatively low in calories and fat. Oily fish are more calorific but again a good source of protein and of omega-3 fatty acids and vitamins A and D. Official advice is that we should all eat at least two portions of fish a week and one of these should be of oily fish.

Here are some examples of each type:

White fish: cod, coley, haddock, hake, halibut, monkfish, plaice, sea bass, skate, sole, whiting.

Oily fish: anchovies, carp, eel, herring, mackerel, salmon, sardines, swordfish, trout, tuna.

SHELLFISH

These are not fish at all but different types of water-dwelling animals, such as mussels, clams, oysters, lobsters, prawns, crabs and scallops. Most have a shell or hard external skeleton. Squid, cuttlefish and octopus are related to mussels and clams but do not have a shell.

COOKING SHELLFISH

I love cooking and eating shellfish but you do have to be careful. Check shellfish such as mussels and clams over carefully before cooking and discard any that look damaged or don't close when tapped sharply. Once the clams or mussels are cooked, throw out any that don't open. I prefer to err on the side of caution here – it's just not worth the risk.

Squid, cuttlefish and octopus are becoming much more common in our shops and all are delicious to eat. If you're nervous about cleaning them, ask your fishmonger to do this for you. They are all best cooked quickly and briefly, or slowly for a long time. Anything in between is likely to result in tough flesh.

You can buy cooked crab, but it is worth cooking your own if you can – it is far better. Don't overcook crab. I think that about 20 minutes per kilo is about right.

FROZEN SEAFOOD

Most fish sold frozen is cleaned, filleted and frozen right on the boat within a few hours of the catch, preserving its freshness. Frozen fish in UK shops comes primarily from Alaska, the North Atlantic and Asia.

Buy frozen fish or seafood where you know the turnover is brisk. Check that the packages look fresh and unbroken. Once frozen fish is in the distribution chain, the recommended storage life is usually three months.

To thaw frozen fish or seafood, leave it to defrost slowly in the fridge for 24 hours. If you're in a hurry, you can run the tightly wrapped fish under COLD water. Cook it as soon as possible to minimize the loss of juices.

If you freeze fish yourself, don't keep it too long. White fish can be kept for up to three months, but oily fish is best used within three weeks as the oil starts to turn rancid and doesn't taste good.

CHILLED MELON SOUP WITH CRAB SALAD

A delightfully refreshing dish, this is just right for a summer lunch and really easy to prepare. Do be sure to use really ripe melons, though. If you like, you could make the salad with cooked prawns instead of crab.

SERVES 4

Chilled melon soup
2 very ripe cantaloupe
   melons
juice of 1 lemon
50g crème fraîche
fine sea salt

Crab salad
125g fresh white crabmeat
1 banana shallot, peeled
   and very finely diced
1 Granny Smith apple,
   peeled, cored and
   finely diced
2 tbsp finely chopped
   parsley
zest and juice of 1 lemon
1 tsp wholegrain mustard
2 tbsp crème fraîche
a few snipped chives,
   to garnish

1 First make the soup. Halve the melons, remove and discard the seeds, then cut the flesh into rough chunks. Place these in a blender with the lemon juice and blitz – you'll need to do this in batches. Pass the mixture through a fine sieve into a bowl.

2 Take 2 tablespoons of the blitzed melon and stir it into the crème fraîche to loosen, then fold the crème fraîche into the rest of the melon soup. Chill the soup in the fridge until needed.

3 Carefully pick through the crabmeat to make sure no bits of shell remain. Place the crabmeat in a bowl and mix with the remaining salad ingredients. Season to taste with salt.

4 To serve, ladle the soup into bowls and add some crab salad on top. Sprinkle with snipped chives.

133

FISH &
SHELLFISH

SEARED SALMON WITH SAUCE VIERGE

Serve this in the summer when fresh herbs are at their tastiest. It makes a really quick, easy and delicious supper and you can use whatever kind of fish you fancy. Just adjust the cooking time according to the thickness of the fillets. Ask your fishmonger to scale the fish for you.

SERVES 4

4 x 180g salmon fillets,
   skin scaled
1 tbsp rapeseed oil
60g butter
juice of 1 lemon

Sauce vierge
150ml extra virgin
   olive oil
1 tbsp small capers,
   drained
3 tbsp chopped
   flatleaf parsley
3 tbsp chopped coriander
3 tbsp finely snipped
   chives
12 basil leaves, chopped
3 plum tomatoes, skinned,
   seeded and diced
juice of 1 lemon
fine sea salt and
   black pepper

1 First make the sauce vierge, which can be served warm or cold. For a warm sauce, put all the ingredients into a small pan, bring it to a simmer, then set aside. For a cold sauce, just put all the ingredients into a bowl and mix well. Season the warm or cold sauce with salt and pepper.

2 Season the salmon all over with salt. Heat the oil in a frying pan and place the fish, skin side down, in the pan. Turn the heat down to medium and cook the salmon for about 4 minutes until the skin is golden brown and crisp.

3 Reduce the heat to low, turn the fish over and add the butter and lemon juice. Cook for a further 3 minutes. Serve with the warm or cold sauce vierge.

🍴 COOK'S TIP 🍴

To skin and seed tomatoes, put them in a pan of boiling water for 30 seconds. Remove them with a slotted spoon and put them in a bowl of cold water, then peel off the skins. They will come away easily. Cut the tomatoes into quarters, then cut out the seeds with a knife and discard.

GRATIN OF SMOKED HADDOCK

I adore this rich, creamy dish, which is such a good way of using lovely undyed smoked haddock. It is a bit decadent, I admit, and if you want to take things a step further, you could serve some fingers of toasted brioche to dip into the sauce. It is very filling and this recipe does make a generous quantity, so you never know – there might be some left over to heat up and enjoy the next day.

SERVES 4

800g undyed smoked
    haddock
450ml whole milk
60g butter
450g leeks, white
    parts only, cut into
    1cm squares
60g plain flour
150ml double cream
pinch of flaked sea salt
200g Gruyère
    cheese, grated

1 Place the smoked haddock in a pan, cover it with the milk and set the pan over a medium heat. Bring the milk to a simmer and gently poach the haddock for 3–5 minutes. Remove the pan from the heat and let the fish cool slightly, then take it out, remove any skin and bones and flake the flesh, allowing the juices to drain. Set the fish aside. Pass the milk through a fine sieve and set it aside for later.

2 Melt the butter in a pan, add the leeks and soften them over a low heat. It's important to get the leeks really soft without letting them brown. Once the leeks are soft, add the flour and cook gently for 30 seconds, then add the reserved milk from cooking the haddock and 50ml of the cream and stir until the sauce thickens. Continue cooking the sauce for a few minutes, then add the flaked fish, taking care not to break it up too much. Season with the salt.

3 Tip the mixture into a medium-sized gratin dish, making sure there is a good 2cm at the top for adding the rest of the cream and the cheese. Allow it to cool to room temperature. Preheat the oven to 200°C/Fan 180°C/Gas 6.

4 Pour the rest of the cream on top, then sprinkle over the Gruyère cheese. Put the dish into the oven and bake for 20 minutes until golden brown on the top. Serve at once.

SPAGHETTI ALLE VONGOLE

February is peak season for shellfish, such as clams and mussels, and I love them all, particularly our native British clams. I always buy extra, as I think you can never have too many clams. It is nice to remove the shells from about half the clams before serving so people aren't loaded up with shells.

SERVES 4

1kg clams in shells
4 ripe plum tomatoes
3 tbsp olive oil, plus
    extra for the pasta
350g dried spaghetti
2 fat garlic cloves, peeled
    and finely chopped
1 small or ½ large
    fresh red chilli,
    finely chopped
150ml white wine
4 tbsp chopped parsley,
    to serve
fine sea salt and
    black pepper

1 Sort through the clams and discard any that are damaged or don't close when given a tap. My motto is 'if in doubt, throw it out', as it's just not worth the risk of eating a bad one. Rinse the clams in several changes of cold water to remove any sand and grit.

2 To skin and seed the tomatoes, put them in a pan of boiling water for 30 seconds. Remove them with a slotted spoon and put them in bowl of cold water, then peel off the skins. They will come away easily. Cut the tomatoes into quarters, remove the seeds and discard, then finely chop the flesh.

3 Bring a large pan of water to the boil. Add a little splash of oil and some salt to the water – the water should be salty. Add the spaghetti, making sure it is completely submerged. Once the pasta is limp, give it a good toss with a pair of tongs so that it doesn't stick together while cooking. Cook for 8–12 minutes, depending on the packet instructions, or until al dente.

4 While the pasta is cooking, start the sauce. Heat the 3 tablespoons of oil in a large pan, add the garlic and chilli, then fry them gently for a few seconds until fragrant. Stir in the chopped tomatoes, then add the rinsed clams and the white wine and bring to the boil. Cover the pan and cook the clams for 3–4 minutes, shaking the pan every now and then until the clams have opened. Discard any clams that haven't opened, then shell half the clams.

5 Drain the spaghetti in a colander and immediately add it to the pan with the clams. Finish with the chopped parsley and add pepper to taste – the natural salt from the clams is usually enough. Serve straight away.

THAI-INSPIRED COCONUT MUSSELS

Mussels are cheap and nutritious and I really like this way of
preparing them – it's a nice change from French-style dishes.
This is all cooked in one pot and makes a very quick meal.

SERVES 4

1kg mussels in shells
2 tbsp vegetable oil
6 spring onions,
    finely sliced
4 garlic cloves, peeled
    and finely chopped
2 lemon grass stalks,
    bruised
2 fresh red chillies, sliced
400ml coconut cream
2 tbsp fish sauce
juice of 2 limes
handful of chopped
    coriander, to garnish

1 Scrub the mussels well, remove the beards and
   scrape off any barnacles. Discard any that are broken
   or don't close when tapped. Don't risk eating a bad
   one – if you're not sure, it's better to throw it away.

2 Heat the oil in a large pan and add the spring onions,
   garlic, lemon grass and most of the sliced chillies –
   keep some back to garnish the dish. Sauté gently for
   2 minutes until everything is softened and fragrant.

3 Add the coconut cream and fish sauce, then bring to
   the boil. Add the mussels, cover the pan and steam
   them for 3 minutes until they've all opened and are
   cooked. Give the pan a good shake every now and
   then. Discard any mussels that don't open.

4 Add the lime juice and serve the mussels in big
   bowls. Garnish with fresh coriander and the
   remaining sliced chillies.

FISH &
SHELLFISH

🍴 COOK'S TIP 🍴

Bruising lemon grass helps to release the
flavour. Keep the stalk whole and bash it with a
knife handle until you can smell the aroma.

BEER-BATTERED COD WITH CRUSHED PEAS

Everyone loves deep-fried fish with a delicious crunchy batter and there's nothing like home-made. It's not difficult, but the trick is to get the batter good and thick enough to coat the fish, and then to make sure your cooking oil is the correct temperature so the fish is cooked through but the batter isn't burnt.

SERVES 4

80g plain flour, plus
   extra for dusting
40g cornflour
1 tsp baking powder
1 tsp malt vinegar,
   plus extra to serve
1 tsp white wine vinegar
100ml cold beer
1 tsp fine sea salt
35ml sparkling water
vegetable oil, for
   deep-frying
4 x 200g cod fillets,
   skinned and pin-boned
flaked sea salt
lemon wedges, to serve

Crushed peas
400g frozen peas
40g butter
pinch of cayenne pepper
1 tsp sugar
fine sea salt and
   white pepper

1 First make the batter. Put the flour, cornflour and baking powder in a bowl, then add the vinegars. Add the beer and whisk until smooth, then add the salt and the sparkling water.

2 Half fill a deep-fat fryer or a large pan with vegetable oil and heat to 180°C. Be careful and never leave the hot oil unattended.

3 Dust the cod in flour and pat off any excess. Dip each piece of cod into the batter, letting some of the excess batter drip off. Place the coated fish straight into the hot oil and cook for 3–4 minutes or until the batter is golden brown and the fish is cooked through. Season with flaked salt and malt vinegar.

4 Meanwhile, cook the peas. Bring a pan of water to the boil, add the peas and cook them for 2 minutes. Drain them well, add the butter, cayenne, sugar and some salt and pepper, then crush. Check the seasoning and serve with the fish. Some chips never go amiss!

FISHERMAN'S STEW

I made the most wonderful Spanish-style fish stew like this when
I was in the show *All at Sea* with Bradley Walsh, and it was a great success.
This is a lovely way to serve fish as it's all cooked in its own juices and
so easy to do. It's an excellent dish for serving to friends – just put the
pot on the table and let everyone dig in and help themselves.

**SERVES 4 VERY
GENEROUSLY**

250g mussels in shells
250g clams in shells
325ml white wine
4 garlic cloves, peeled
   and chopped
2 red peppers
4 tbsp olive oil
½ Spanish onion, peeled
   and finely sliced
large pinch of
   saffron strands
6 tomatoes, quartered
450g new potatoes,
   boiled and left whole
8 raw shelled king prawns
2 medium squid, cleaned
   and cut into rings (use
   tentacles as well)
500g thick haddock
   fillet, skinned and cut
   into large chunks
thinly pared peel of
   1 lemon
about 500ml good
   fish stock
handful of chopped
   flatleaf parsley, to serve
fine sea salt and
   black pepper

1 Scrub the mussels well, remove the beards and scrape off any barnacles. Give the clams a good wash and discard any mussels or clams that are broken or don't close when tapped. Don't risk eating a bad one – if you're not sure, it's better to throw it away.

2 Pour the wine into a large pan with a lid and add half the chopped garlic. Bring the wine to the boil, then add the mussels, cover the pan and cook them for 3 minutes until they open. Remove the mussels with a slotted spoon and put them in a bowl, discarding any that don't open.

3 Add the clams to the pan and cook them, covered, for 2 minutes until they open, then remove them with a slotted spoon and add them to the mussels. Again, discard any that don't open. Strain the wine through a fine sieve and set it aside.

4 Remove the skin of the peppers with a potato peeler, then cut the flesh into thin strips and discard the seeds. Heat the oil in large flameproof casserole dish or even a wok, add the sliced peppers and onion and allow them to soften slowly over a gentle heat. Take your time over this, as it is important for them to be well cooked. Add the strained wine, the saffron and the rest of the garlic. Mix well and bring to a simmer, then turn the heat down.

5 Add the tomatoes, potatoes, prawns, squid, haddock and lemon peel and enough fish stock to cover. Stir well, cover the pan and cook for 10 minutes over a medium heat until everything is done. Remove the lid and season well with salt and pepper, then fold in the mussels and clams and sprinkle with parsley. Serve at once.

SEA BREAM WITH BROWN SHRIMP AND BROWN BUTTER SAUCE

This is based on a Dover sole recipe with a similar sauce and it's an excellent dish for a special occasion. You could also make this with sea bass, which is usually a little cheaper, and if you're worried about the amount of butter, you don't have to add butter to the fish in the pan – although it is delicious.

SERVES 4

1 tbsp rapeseed oil
4 sea bream fillets
60g butter
juice of ½ lemon

Brown shrimp and brown butter sauce
100g butter
juice of 1 lemon
150g brown shrimp
2 tbsp small capers, drained
2 tbsp finely chopped curly parsley
fine sea salt

1 Heat the oil in a frying pan over a medium heat. Put the fillets, skin side down, into the pan and cook them for 2–3 minutes or until the skin is golden brown and crisp. You may need to cook the fish in a couple of batches, depending on the size of your pan. Turn the fillets over, add the butter and lemon juice and cook for a further minute, depending on the thickness of the fish. Remove the fillets from the pan and keep them warm.

2 While the fish is resting, make the sauce in the same pan. Wipe the pan with kitchen paper, then add the butter and melt it over a medium heat until it starts to turn nutty brown. Add the lemon juice, brown shrimp, capers and the parsley, then warm through.

3 Serve the fish fillets on warm plates and pour the brown butter sauce over them. Season to taste with salt and serve at once – perhaps with some lovely Jersey Royal potatoes sprinkled with parsley.

CRISPY CHILLI SQUID WITH THAI SWEET CHILLI SAUCE

This is the most delicious dish and not hard to make. The trick with squid is to cook it for either a short or long time or it can be tough. Here it is just flash-fried, which is perfect. If you like, you could use squid rings instead of whole squid to make things even easier.

SERVES 4 AS A STARTER

Squid
8 small squid with
   tentacles, cleaned
150g plain flour
1 heaped tbsp ground
   white pepper
½ tsp flaked sea salt
4 tbsp vegetable oil
4 spring onions,
   finely sliced
2 fresh red and
   2 fresh green chillies,
   finely sliced
4 garlic cloves, peeled
   and finely sliced
handful of mint,
   chopped, to garnish

Thai sweet chilli sauce
2 large fresh red chillies,
   roughly chopped
20g fresh root
   ginger, peeled and
   finely grated
4 garlic cloves, peeled
   and roughly chopped
finely grated zest of 3
   limes and juice of 2
large bunch of coriander,
   leaves only
150g golden caster sugar
10ml fish sauce
60ml white wine vinegar

1 First make the sauce. Put the chillies, ginger, garlic, lime zest and juice and the coriander in a small food processor and blitz to make a paste. Set it aside.

2 Put the sugar into a pan with 2 tablespoons of water and place the pan over a medium heat. Once the sugar has dissolved, increase the heat and leave until the water has evaporated and the sugar has turned into a light caramel. Meanwhile, heat the fish sauce and vinegar with the chilli paste.

3 When a light caramel has formed, remove the pan from the heat. Stir the heated fish sauce, vinegar and chilli paste into the caramel, then put the pan back over the heat. Simmer the sauce for 30–60 seconds to combine, then remove and leave to cool.

4 Take a squid and, using a sharp knife, slice the body open. Place it on a board with the inside facing up. Gently score the flesh by running the knife diagonally down the squid, making sure not to go all the way through the flesh. Do the same in the opposite direction to make a diamond pattern. Score the rest of the squid in the same way. Keep the tentacles separate.

5 Put the flour, pepper and salt in a bowl and mix. Dip each squid into the flour and coat well, tapping off any excess. Flour the tentacles in the same way.

6 Place a frying pan over a high heat and add the oil. When the oil is smoking hot, add the squid, scored side down, and the tentacles, then cook for 1 minute. Toss the pan and add the spring onions, chillies and garlic, then toss again and cook for a further minute. Garnish with the mint and serve with the chilli sauce.

SEA BASS EN PAPILLOTE WITH THAI COUSCOUS

If you're a bit nervous about cooking fish, this is a great dish to try. Everything is cooked together en papillote (in a parcel), which seals in all the flavour and makes for an absolutely delicious result. And because the fish gently steams in the parcel, you're not likely to overcook it. Ask your fishmonger to scale the fish.

SERVES 4

200g couscous
250ml just-boiled water
1 tbsp vegetable oil, plus
    extra for greasing
2 shallots, peeled and
    finely chopped
2 garlic cloves, peeled
    and finely chopped
1 tsp ground cumin
1 tsp ground coriander
2 lime leaves, thinly
    shredded
2 lemon grass stalks,
    spilt lengthways
1 fresh red or green chilli,
    seeded and chopped
15g fresh root ginger,
    peeled and finely
    chopped
½ tsp ground turmeric
juice of 1 lime
1 tbsp fish sauce
1 red pepper, seeded
    and diced
225g spinach, stalks
    removed and
    leaves torn
large bunch of coriander,
    stalks trimmed and
    leaves chopped
4 sea bass fillets, scaled
    and pin-boned
fine sea salt

1 First put the couscous in a roomy dish and pour the boiling water over it. Cover the bowl with cling film and set it aside while you prepare the stir-fry.

2 Heat the oil in a wok or a large heavy-based frying pan over a medium-high heat. Add the shallots and garlic and fry them for 2 minutes until softened but not browned. Then add the cumin, coriander, lime leaves, lemon grass, chilli, ginger, turmeric and lime juice and stir-fry for 1 minute. Stir in the fish sauce and cook for 2 minutes, then add the red pepper and cook for 3 minutes more. Finally, add the spinach and fresh coriander, then set aside.

3 By now the couscous should have absorbed all the liquid. Gently fluff it up with a fork and stir in the cooked mixture, removing the lemon grass. Preheat the oven to 200°C/Fan 180°C/Gas 6.

4 Cut 4 pieces of baking paper measuring about 30cm square and grease them lightly with oil. Divide the couscous mixture between them, placing it on one side of each square. Place a sea bass fillet, skin side up, on top of each pile of couscous and season with salt. Fold over the paper and scrunch the edges together to make parcels – a bit like a Cornish pasty.

5 Place the parcels on a baking tray and bake for about 15 minutes or until the fish is cooked through and the couscous is piping hot. Serve at once. (If you don't have any baking paper, you can use foil instead, but you'll need a double layer for each parcel.)

LEMON SOLE WITH TOASTED HERB AND PARMESAN CRUMBS

This is a nice show-off dish to prepare for friends. It looks really fancy but it's easy to do – you can get it all ready in advance, then just pop it in the oven when it's time to eat. Lovely served with Green Herb Couscous (see page 113). Ask your fishmonger to fillet and skin the soles for you.

SERVES 4

50g butter
vegetable oil, for frying
    and greasing
75g panko breadcrumbs
1 banana shallot, peeled
    and finely chopped
2 garlic cloves, peeled
    and finely chopped
50g Parmesan cheese,
    finely grated
zest of 1 lemon
1 tbsp finely chopped
    parsley
1 tbsp finely chopped
    chervil
1 tbsp finely chopped
    chives
2 large lemon soles,
    filleted and skinned
fine sea salt

1 Place a frying pan over a medium heat and add the butter with a few drops of oil. Once the butter has melted, add the breadcrumbs, season with salt, then cook and stir until the breadcrumbs are golden brown. Tip the breadcrumbs on to a cloth or kitchen paper to remove any excess butter.

2 Wipe the frying pan clean and place it back over a medium heat. Add a tablespoon of oil and the shallot and garlic, then cook them for a couple of minutes until softened. Leave them to cool, then mix the shallot and garlic with the toasted breadcrumbs, Parmesan, lemon zest and the chopped herbs. Preheat the oven to 200°C/Fan 180°C/Gas 6.

3 Line a roasting tin with greaseproof paper and drizzle it with a teaspoon of oil. Cut the lemon sole fillets in half crossways, so you have 8 pieces. Trim the edges so that they are all the same length. Place a piece of lemon sole in the tin and top with some of the breadcrumb mix. Place another piece of sole on top and cover with more of the breadcrumb mix. Repeat to make 4 lemon sole 'sandwiches'.

4 Place the tin in the preheated oven for 5–7 minutes until the fish is cooked through and the topping is golden brown. Serve at once.

FISH & SHELLFISH

CURRIED SCALLOPS WITH CAULIFLOWER, APRICOTS AND SULTANAS

I always buy hand-dived scallops, as I have seen the damage caused
by the trawling method. I would rather pay more and have scallops
as an occasional treat. Cauliflower, curry and scallops have a
real affinity and this is an utterly delicious dish. Do try it.

SERVES 4 AS A STARTER

2 tbsp curry powder
4 large scallops, trimmed
2 tbsp vegetable oil
25g butter
juice of ½ lemon

Cauliflower
1 small cauliflower
50g butter
1 tsp vegetable oil
2 banana shallots, peeled
    and finely diced
1 garlic clove, peeled
    and finely chopped
1 tsp curry powder
1 tsp ground coriander
1 tsp ground cumin
1 large baking potato,
    peeled and cut
    into 1cm dice
40g dried apricots,
    chopped
40g sultanas
zest and juice of 1 lemon
2 tbsp chopped coriander
1 tbsp chopped mint
fine sea salt

Garnish
2 tbsp almonds, toasted in
    a dry pan and chopped
2 tbsp chopped coriander

1 Start by preparing the cauliflower. Preheat the oven
to 200°C/Fan 180°C/Gas 6. Remove the outer leaves
from the cauliflower, then, using a small sharp knife,
cut the cauliflower into large florets about 3cm wide.

2 Melt the butter with the vegetable oil in a flameproof
casserole dish, then add the shallots and garlic. Cook
over a gentle heat for 5 minutes or until the shallots
start to brown. Add the spices and continue to cook
gently for 2 minutes, stirring all the time so that the
spices don't stick. Stir in the diced potato, coating it
in the spices, then add 150ml of water and some salt.
Cook gently over a medium heat for 5 minutes.

3 Stir in the cauliflower florets, dried fruit and the
lemon zest and juice, then place the casserole dish
in the preheated oven and cook for 8–10 minutes, or
until the cauliflower and potatoes are tender and the
water has reduced. The mixture should be fairly dry.
Stir in the chopped herbs and taste for seasoning,
adding more salt and lemon juice if you think it's
needed. Place the cauliflower in a serving bowl and
garnish with the toasted nuts and chopped coriander.

4 Now cook the scallops. Mix the curry powder and
a teaspoon of salt in a bowl and dip the flat side of
each scallop into the curry seasoning. Heat the oil in
a frying pan until almost smoking, add the scallops,
seasoned side down, and cook them for 1 minute until
golden brown. Add the butter, then the lemon juice
and baste the scallops. Turn the scallops over and
remove the pan from the heat. Allow the scallops to
sit in the warm butter and lemon juice for 1 minute,
off the heat. Serve at once, placing each scallop on a
helping of cauliflower. Drizzle with the cooking juices.

POULTRY & GAME

*The chapter begins with the basics, then progresses, skill by skill,
recipe by recipe, up to showpiece dishes that really wow.*

A GOOD ROAST CHICKEN HAS ALWAYS BEEN one of my family's favourite meals. It can be simple – just flavoured with a few herbs and served with a salad – or a real feast with stuffing, gravy and roast potatoes. Either way, a chicken dinner takes some beating. I also enjoy duck and turkey as a special treat, and game birds, such as pheasant and partridge. In this chapter, you will find recipes ranging from a very easy lemon-flavoured roast chicken to a spectacular four-bird roast, worthy of the grandest celebration.

Chicken is so versatile and partners well with a multitude of herbs and spices. It's loved the world over and is the basis of an astonishing array of classic dishes from curries and casseroles to pies and pilafs. Chicken adapts to almost anything.

You'll notice a big difference in price between different types of chicken. If you can afford it, a free-range bird really does have a far superior flavour and texture, and I do like to know that my chicken has lived a reasonable life, with some access to the outdoors. If, however, you're feeding a family and money is tight, you can still make a good meal with an ordinary supermarket chicken. The vital thing is to cook it carefully, season it well and add plenty of flavour with herbs and spices.

CHICKEN HYGIENE
Chicken can be contaminated with bacteria and although it is perfectly safe to eat when properly cooked, you do need to handle it carefully to avoid cross-contamination. Here are some basic guidelines.
- When you buy chicken, take it out of any plastic wrapping, put it on a plate and cover it with greaseproof paper. Store it at the bottom of the fridge so it can't drip on any other food.
- Never wash raw chicken – you risk spraying the bacteria around.
- When preparing chicken, use a separate chopping board and always wash any utensils that come into contact with the raw chicken thoroughly. Wash your hands well after handling raw chicken and before touching any other foods.
- Do not allow raw chicken to come into contact with any cooked foods.
- Cook chicken thoroughly so no pinkness remains. Ideally, check with a meat thermometer, inserting it into the thickest part of the meat. It should reach 70–75°C.
- Fresh chicken can be frozen, but use it within six months or the texture and flavour deteriorates. I really don't like chicken with freezer burn.

OTHER TYPES OF POULTRY
Duck is delicious and unlike chicken can be served pink – but never rare all the way through. If you don't want to roast a whole duck, the breasts are easy to cook. Just season the breasts with fine salt and put them in a cold pan, skin side down. Cook over a low heat to render the fat and crisp up the skin (see my recipe on page 172).

Guinea fowl has a flavour in between chicken and game. It's not quite as easy

CHICKEN CUTS

Wing

Thigh

Breast

Wishbone

Drumstick

to cook as chicken but delicious when you get it right – try my recipe with gin on page 169. Guinea fowl is always best cooked with some moisture or steamed to counteract any dryness.

In the autumn and winter game season, do try birds such as pheasant and grouse. Early in the season they can be simply roasted. Older birds are best braised or casseroled.

CHICKEN CUTS

When roasting chicken for the family I often buy two small birds instead of one big one. That way everyone can get their choice of breast or dark meat. If you want chicken pieces, it's far cheaper to buy a whole chicken than packages of chicken joints. Ask the butcher to joint the chicken for you, and if you don't need it all right away, wrap the pieces well and freeze them for another day.

Breasts: For many people, the breast – the white meat – is their favourite part of the chicken. I like breast for dishes such as

chicken korma and chicken Kiev, but do take care as it can be dry if overcooked. A useful tip is to keep the little fillets from the breasts and freeze them until you have enough for a stir-fry.

Wings: There's not much meat on a chicken wing but loads of flavour. They are great roasted on the barbecue and respond well to marinades and spicy flavours.

Legs: The whole leg – comprising thigh and drumstick – is the dark meat and excellent for casseroles and braises.

Thighs: For me, these are the tastiest, most succulent parts of the chicken. They're cheaper than breast and easier to cook, as they stay juicy and delicious even when cooked for a long time. I like to cook thighs on the bone in tray bakes or you can bone them and cook on a griddle or barbecue.

Drumsticks: Also cheap and easy to cook but not as good as thighs, in my opinion.

Wishbone: When I was a child, we always used to dry the wishbone on the windowsill then pull it to see who would get their heart's desire!

LEMON-CURED CHICKEN

This is a simple but delicious roast, but you do need to start preparations
the day before by rubbing the chicken with the lemon mixture. It really
is worth doing this, as it makes a big difference to the texture of the meat.
Lovely served with Crushed New Potatoes (see page 75) and some salad.

SERVES 4

2 tbsp runny honey
2 tbsp soft brown sugar
2 lemons
1 tbsp flaked sea salt
1 tsp black peppercorns,
    crushed
olive oil, for drizzling
1 x 1.5kg chicken

1 The day before you want to cook the chicken,
mix together the honey, sugar, zest of the lemons,
salt and peppercorns. Rub the mixture all over the
chicken, then put the chicken in a bowl, cover and
leave it in the fridge for 24 hours. Turn the chicken
every 4 hours or whenever possible.

2 Preheat the oven to 170°C/Fan 150°/Gas 3½. Remove
the chicken from the fridge and discard any liquid.
Put the chicken in a roasting tin and throw the lemon
halves in too if you like. Drizzle the chicken with oil
and roast in the preheated oven for about 1 hour and
20 minutes, or until the juices run clear. If you have
a digital meat thermometer, put it in the thickest part
of the leg – the meat should reach 70°C. If you find
the top is going too brown, cover it with some foil.

3 Once the chicken is done, remove it from the oven
and leave it to rest for 20 minutes before carving.

🍸 COOK'S TIP 🍸
You can finish this chicken on the barbecue
if you like. Cook it in the oven as above for
an hour, then put it on the barbecue, over
a medium heat, for 15–20 minutes. Check
that it's perfectly cooked before serving.

DEVILLED CHICKEN LIVERS ON TOASTED CIABATTA

This is my take on devilled kidneys but made with chicken livers, which are cheap and readily available. I like to spread the toast with lashings of butter before adding the livers, but that's up to you. Delish!

SERVES 4

500g fresh chicken
    livers (about 450g
    once trimmed)
plain flour, for dusting
big pinch of chilli powder
1 tsp Worcestershire
    sauce
1 tsp mustard powder
1 tsp tomato purée
1 tsp soy sauce
1 rounded tsp
    redcurrant jelly
150ml chicken stock
40g butter
1 ciabatta loaf
fine sea salt and
    black pepper

1 Trim the chicken livers, removing the white sinew and cutting out any green bits.

2 Put the flour in a bowl and season it with salt and chilli powder. Drop in the livers and toss them in the flour, then shake off any excess.

3 Mix the Worcestershire sauce, mustard powder, tomato purée, soy sauce and redcurrant jelly in a bowl. Add half the chicken stock and mix again.

4 Melt the butter in a large frying pan over a medium heat. Add the floured livers and fry them for about 1 minute on each side.

5 Add the sauce mixture and stir well to coat the livers. Season with salt and pepper to taste and cook for a minute. If the mixture seems to be getting dry, add the rest of the stock.

6 Slice the ciabatta in half crossways, then slice each half horizontally to make 4 pieces. Toast the ciabatta, then pile the devilled livers on top.

CHICKEN KORMA

Chicken korma was voted Britain's favourite curry in a recent survey and is practically our national dish! There are so many versions and this is my take. It's not hard to do and makes a perfect Saturday night family feast.

SERVES 4

4 boneless chicken
     breasts, skinned
2 tbsp vegetable oil,
     plus extra if needed
4 banana shallots,
     peeled and sliced
6 garlic cloves, peeled
     and crushed
25g fresh root
     ginger, peeled and
     finely grated
seeds from 10 cardamom
     pods, ground
2 tbsp ground cumin
2 tbsp ground coriander
4 whole cloves
1 tbsp ground turmeric
2 bay leaves, scrunched
bunch of coriander, stalks
     finely chopped, leaves
     roughly chopped,
50g butter
2 tbsp plain flour
2 tsp golden caster sugar
400ml can of coconut milk
juice of 1 lemon
fine sea salt

1   Cut each chicken breast into 6 pieces all about the same size and season them with salt. Heat the oil in a large, heavy-based pan, add the chicken pieces and fry them on all sides over a medium heat until golden brown. It's best to do this in batches so you don't overcrowd the pan or the meat will steam and not brown. Remove each batch of chicken from the pan and set it aside.

2   If the pan seems dry, add a splash more oil, then the shallots, garlic and ginger. Cook them over a low heat for about 5 minutes until softened and browned. Then stir in the spices, bay leaves and the chopped coriander stalks. Cook them for 5 minutes until you can smell the lovely aromas, stirring all the time so that the spices don't catch on the bottom of the pan.

3   Add the butter and let it melt over the spices. Stir in the flour and sugar and cook for 2 minutes, then add 150ml of cold water. Bring to the boil and reduce until there is no water left, scraping up any sticky bits from the pan.

4   Remove the bay leaves and blend the mixture in a food processor until it is as smooth as possible. You can use this paste straight away, chill it for up to 3 days or freeze it. Be sure to defrost thoroughly before using.

5   If using the paste immediately, put it back into the pan, add the coconut milk and bring it to a simmer. Add the browned chicken and simmer gently for 5–6 minutes or until the chicken is tender and cooked through – this will depend on the size of the pieces. Once the chicken is done, season it with lemon juice and salt, garnish with the coriander leaves, then serve with Pilau Rice (see page 112).

POULTRY
& GAME

PHEASANT BREASTS WITH WILD MUSHROOM AND TARRAGON PAPPARDELLE

I love seasonal food and I always make this dish when pheasant is in the shops. At other times, you could use chicken or guinea fowl breasts, but you will need to cook them for longer. Pappardelle are broad ribbons of pasta that work very well with rich sauces like this one.

SERVES 4

50g butter
olive oil, for frying
1 garlic clove, peeled
    and crushed
4 pheasant breasts,
    skinned
400g pappardelle pasta
snipped chives, to garnish
flaked sea salt and
    black pepper

Sauce
2 tbsp olive oil
1 medium onion, peeled
    and finely chopped
4 rashers of streaky
    bacon, finely chopped
450g celeriac, peeled
    and finely diced
250g mixed wild
    mushrooms, cleaned
    and sliced
1 tsp fresh or dried thyme
60g fresh tarragon or
    1 tbsp dried tarragon
30g butter
150ml wine (optional)
300ml chicken or
    pheasant stock
100ml double cream

1 Place a frying pan over a medium heat, add half the butter, a splash of oil and the garlic, then cook for a couple of minutes. Add the pheasant breasts, cook them for 2 minutes, then turn them over and cook for a further 2 minutes. Turn the breasts again, then add the rest of the butter, season well and continue to cook and baste for about 2 minutes. The pheasant should be cooked through but still slightly pink in the middle. Do not overcook. Remove the breasts from the pan, cover them with foil and set them aside to rest.

2 For the sauce, add the 2 tablespoons of oil to the same pan and place it over a high heat. Add the onion and bacon and cook until golden brown, then add the celeriac, mushrooms, thyme and tarragon. Add the butter and continue cooking for 1 minute, then pour in the wine, if using, and continue to cook until it has reduced to a tablespoonful. Add the stock and cook until it has reduced by half. Pour in the cream, simmer for a couple of minutes, then season well. Take the pan off the heat, cover it with a lid or foil and set aside to keep warm.

3 Meanwhile, bring a large pan of water to the boil and cook the pappardelle according to the packet instructions. Drain it, then tip it back into the pan. Add half the celeriac and wild mushroom sauce, toss it all well and season again.

4 Slice the pheasant breasts, then mix them with the pasta and add the rest of the sauce. Garnish with snipped chives and serve at once.

HARISSA-SPICED CHICKEN THIGHS WITH TOMATO AND CANNELLINI BEANS

Yes, there are a lot of ingredients here, but the paste and the rub simply
need mixing quickly and the rest is easy. Thighs are my favourite
part of the chicken and I like to keep them on the bone for juicy
meat that never goes dry. This is a tasty meal that everyone enjoys.
And you will have some harissa paste left for another day.

SERVES 4

8 large chicken thighs,
   bone in but skinned
3 tbsp olive oil
400ml chicken stock.
1 tsp tomato purée
½ quantity of harissa
   paste or to taste
4 dried figs, chopped
16 cherry tomatoes,
   cut in half
400g can of cannellini
   beans, drained
   and rinsed
large handful of fresh
   coriander, chopped
fine sea salt

Harissa paste
100g fresh red chillies
1 tbsp olive oil
3 garlic cloves, peeled
1 tbsp chopped coriander
¼ tsp ground cumin
1½ tbsp tomato purée
1½ tbsp sugar

Spice rub
2 tsp ground cumin
3 tsp ground coriander
½ tsp grated nutmeg
1 tbsp peanut oil

1 To make the harissa paste, remove the seeds from
   the chillies, then blend all the ingredients in a food
   processor with a good pinch of salt to make a nice
   chunky paste.

2 Mix the spices for the rub in a bowl, then stir in the
   oil and a teaspoon of salt. Rub this mixture all over
   the chicken thighs and leave them, covered, for at
   least 30 minutes, or overnight in the fridge.

3 When you're ready to cook the chicken, heat the
   oil in a large frying pan, add the chicken thighs
   and brown them on all sides. Add the chicken
   stock, tomato purée, harissa, figs and tomatoes.
   Bring to the boil, turn the heat down and simmer
   for 15 minutes. Turn the chicken over halfway
   through the cooking time.

4 Add the cannellini beans and cook for a further
   20 minutes. Check the seasoning, then toss in the
   chopped coriander. Serve with rice. Store the rest
   of the harissa in a covered bowl or jar in the fridge.

SUN-BLUSHED TOMATO CHICKEN KIEV

This is a variation on the usual chicken Kiev with a delicious
tomatoey filling. It is a decadent dish and one for a special treat,
but it is well worth trying. Serve with a green salad.

SERVES 4

100g sun-blushed
  tomatoes, drained well
2 large garlic cloves,
  peeled and finely
  chopped
40g butter, at room
  temperature
1 thyme sprig
2 tbsp roughly
  chopped parsley
150g plain flour
200g panko breadcrumbs,
  blitzed in a food
  processor until fine
3 eggs, beaten
4 small boneless chicken
  breasts, skinned
vegetable oil, for frying
fine sea salt and
  black pepper

1 Put the tomatoes in a food processor with the garlic,
   butter, thyme and parsley and blitz to form a paste.
   Divide this into 4 portions and put them in the freezer
   for 30 minutes. This makes the stuffing easier to use.

2 Put the flour and blitzed breadcrumbs in separate
   shallow bowls and beat the eggs in a third bowl.
   Season the flour with salt and pepper.

3 Take a chicken breast and make a small slit in one
   side. Work into the breast to make a hole big enough
   to fill with a portion of stuffing, but be careful not
   to cut all the way through. Season the flesh inside,
   then push the stuffing right in. Brush the rim with a
   little of the beaten egg, then seal. Prepare the other
   chicken breasts in the same way.

4 Carefully dip each chicken breast into the flour and
   lightly dredge, then dip it into the egg and finally
   into the breadcrumbs, then repeat the egg and
   breadcrumbs so each breast is double-coated.

5 Half fill a deep-fat fryer or a large pan with oil. Heat
   to 160°C and cook the chicken Kievs, a couple at a
   time, for 10–12 minutes or until golden brown and
   cooked through. Alternatively, you can bake the
   chicken in a preheated oven (200°C/Fan 180°C/Gas 6)
   for 40 minutes.

THE SHRAGERS' CHICKEN AND POTATO PIE

I've created many versions of my family's classic pie recipe. I love it, my family love it – it's a winner. It's great hot or cold, wonderful for a picnic and an excellent pie to take along to a party.

SERVES 4

80g butter, plus extra
    for greasing
500g potatoes (Maris
    Pipers are good), peeled
    and very thinly sliced
2 skinless, boneless
    chicken breasts,
    cut into thin strips
2 tbsp chopped
    tarragon leaves
2 tbsp snipped chives
1 x 500g packet of
    puff pastry
plain flour, for dusting
2 egg yolks, lightly beaten
150ml double cream
    (optional)
fine sea salt and
    black pepper

1 Melt half the butter in a frying pan. Add the potatoes and turn them in the butter over a gentle heat until cooked. Don't let them brown. Place the potatoes in a large bowl and leave them to cool.

2 Add the remaining butter to the pan and add the strips of chicken. Keep turning them over a steady heat for a few minutes until they are just cooked. Add the herbs, then tip the contents of the pan into the bowl with the potatoes. Season well, then leave the mixture to cool.

3 Preheat the oven to 200°C/Fan 180°C/Gas 6. Cut the pastry into 2 pieces – one-third and two-thirds. On a floured worktop, roll the smaller piece into a circle about 28cm in diameter and put it on a lightly greased baking sheet. Brush the edges with some of the beaten egg yolk, then pile the chicken and potato mixture in the middle.

4 Roll the rest of the pastry into a larger circle, about 38cm in diameter, and use it to cover the pie, sealing and crimping the edges inwards. Cut a little circle (about 6cm in diameter) in the pastry at the top to make a lid, leaving the lid in place. Brush the pie all over with the rest of the egg yolk. Put the pie in the preheated oven and bake it for 20 minutes. Turn the heat down to 180°C/Fan 160°C/Gas 4 and cook the pie for another 30 minutes. If the top starts to get too brown, reduce the oven temperature slightly.

5 When the pie is almost ready, pour the cream, if using, into a pan and bring it to the boil. Take the pie out and remove the pastry lid. Pour in the cream, while putting a knife into the hole to break up the filling so the cream can flow into the gaps. Replace the lid and bake the pie for another 10 minutes.

ROAST GUINEA FOWL WITH SULTANAS, BACON AND GIN

Guinea fowl can be dry but this cooking method keeps it moist and succulent and very tasty. It's based on an Italian recipe with Vin Santo, but I like to use gin instead. There are so many lovely varieties of gin available at the moment and it gives the meat a wonderful slightly gamey flavour. Serve with Boulangère or Dauphinoise Potatoes (see pages 104–5) or salad.

SERVES 4

40g thyme sprigs,
    finely chopped
leaves from 2 rosemary
    sprigs, chopped
4 rashers of smoked
    streaky bacon, chopped
2 tbsp extra virgin
    olive oil
juice and zest of 2 lemons
1 large guinea fowl
handful of sultanas
1 tsp juniper berries
100ml dry gin (or
    extra stock)
100ml chicken stock
fine sea salt and
    black pepper

1 Line a roasting tin with foil, make sure there is plenty hanging over the edges so you can wrap up the fowl. Preheat the oven to 200°C/Fan 180°C/Gas 6.

2 Mix the chopped herbs with the bacon, oil, lemon juice and zest, then season with salt and pepper. Season the guinea fowl inside and out, then rub it all over with the herb and bacon mixture – rub some inside the bird too. Sprinkle over the sultanas and juniper berries and pour over the gin, if using, and the stock. (If you don't want to use gin, just add extra stock.) Bring up the edges of the foil and wrap the bird tightly.

3 Roast the guinea fowl in the preheated oven for 45 minutes, then open up the foil and roast for another 25 minutes until the skin is nice and golden. Remove the guinea fowl from the oven and leave it to rest for 15 minutes.

4 Carve off the breasts and legs and serve with all the lovely juices.

ROAST DUCK WITH PANCAKES, PLUM SAUCE AND SESAME SEED CUCUMBER

This is my version of Peking duck, which all my family love.
You can make the pancakes and plum sauce in advance, or to
make this super-speedy, use some shop-bought hoisin sauce and
pancakes, which you can find online or in supermarkets.

SERVES 4

4 tbsp runny honey,
  dissolved in 2
  tbsp water
2 tbsp dark soy sauce
1 medium duck

Plum sauce
500g plums, stoned
  and chopped
2 star anise
1 cinnamon stick
40g golden caster sugar
2 tbsp cider vinegar
2 tbsp dark soy sauce
2 tsp English mustard
  powder
1 tsp fine sea salt

Sesame seed cucumber
1 cucumber, peeled
1 tsp fine sea salt
2 tbsp sesame seeds
1 tbsp golden caster sugar
½ fresh red chilli,
  finely chopped
2 spring onions, trimmed
  and finely chopped
1 garlic clove, peeled
  and finely chopped
1 tbsp finely chopped
  fresh root ginger

Continued...

1 Preheat the oven to 220°C/Fan 200°C/Gas 7. Mix
   together the dissolved honey and soy sauce and
   brush the duck all over with the mixture. Place
   the duck on a rack in a roasting tin and roast it for
   1½ hours, basting once or twice. Check to make sure
   the duck is not getting too brown and if it is, cover
   it loosely with foil.

2 For the plum sauce, put all the ingredients in a pan,
   cover and cook over a medium heat for 5 minutes.
   Remove the lid and cook for a further 10–15 minutes.
   Take out the star anise and cinnamon, tip the mixture
   into a food processor and blitz to a purée. Set aside.

3 For the cucumber, slice the cucumber into long strips
   with a potato peeler or mandolin. Put the strips in a
   colander, sprinkle with the salt and leave for 1 hour.
   Drain them well and pat dry. Brown the sesame seeds
   in a dry pan over a medium heat, then tip them into a
   bowl and leave to cool. Add the remaining ingredients,
   except the cucumber, to the bowl and mix well, then
   carefully add the cucumber strips. Handle them very
   gently so they don't break.

4 For the pancakes, put the flour, chilli powder, if using,
   and salt into a large bowl. Slowly add the water,
   mixing all the time. Add 2 teaspoons of oil, then mix
   to form a smooth dough. Divide the dough into 2.
   On a worktop dusted with flour, roll out each piece
   into a cylinder shape, then cut each cylinder into 12.

5 Roll each piece into a ball, then flatten them. Take one
   disc, brush it with oil and place another on top, then
   roll them into a circle about 5mm thick. Repeat to
   make the remaining pairs of pancakes. Heat a frying

2 tbsp finely chopped
    coriander
zest and juice of 1 lime
1 tbsp dark soy sauce
1 tbsp sesame seed oil

Pancakes
500g plain flour, plus
    extra for dusting
½ tsp chilli powder
    (optional)
1 tsp fine sea salt
400ml just-boiled water
50ml vegetable oil

pan and fry the pancakes, one pair at a time, for a minute on each side. Once cooled, peel the pancakes apart and leave them covered with a damp cloth until required. When you're ready to cook them, put them in a steamer and steam for a few minutes over a pan of simmering water, or wrap them in foil and warm them through in a low oven.

6 Carve the duck and arrange it on a serving dish. Put it on the table with the pancakes, plum sauce and cucumber. To eat, spread about a teaspoon of the plum sauce into the centre of a pancake, add a strip of cucumber and some duck, then roll up the pancake. Turn up the bottom edge to prevent the contents from falling out.

🍴 COOK'S TIP 🍴

The pancakes freeze very well. Just put a piece of greaseproof paper between each one so it is easy to remove the quantity you need. To serve, steam them for a few minutes as above. They are great for wraps as well as for this recipe.

POULTRY
& GAME

DUCK BREASTS WITH PICKLED CHERRIES AND POTATO AND TURNIP GRATIN

An unusual dish, this is easy to prepare and it tastes really special – a good one for serving to friends. You can prepare the cherries well in advance and get the gratin in the oven, then all you have to do at the last minute is cook the duck and you have a beautiful feast. You can make the pickle with fresh cherries, but the jars are convenient and available all year round.

SERVES 4

4 duck breasts
40g butter
fine sea salt and
   black pepper

Pickled cherries
250g morello cherries
   (from a jar)
50ml raspberry vinegar
75ml red wine
125ml red wine vinegar
65g golden caster sugar
thinly pared peel of
   ½ orange
1 small cinnamon stick
2 cloves
8 black peppercorns
½ star anise

Continued...

1 First prepare the cherries. Drain the cherries and put them in a bowl. Place the remaining ingredients into a pan, bring everything to the boil, then turn the heat down and simmer for about 10 minutes. Pour the mixture over the cherries in the bowl, then cover and set aside.

2 For the gratin, heat the oil in a frying pan, then add the onion and cook it until softened. Pour the cream and milk into a separate pan and add the garlic. Bring the milk and cream to the boil, then turn off the heat and leave to infuse. Season the cream generously so it tastes salty. Preheat the oven to 170°C/Fan 150°C/Gas 3½.

3 Butter an ovenproof gratin dish. Add layers of turnips, potatoes and cooked onion to the dish, then pour over some of the cream mixture. Repeat until you have added all the ingredients, pressing down each layer as you go. Dot the butter over the top.

4 Place the dish in the preheated oven and bake for 1½ hours. Remove and press the gratin down with the base of another dish, then put it back in the oven for about another 20 minutes. To test if the gratin is ready, insert a knife into the middle – if it goes in easily, the gratin is done. Set it aside to rest for about 10 minutes.

5 While the gratin is resting, cook the duck breasts. Using a sharp knife, make 5 incisions in the skin of each duck breast. Put the breasts, skin side down, in a cold non-stick frying pan. Slowly increase the heat and cook the breasts for about 6 minutes until the

Potato and turnip gratin

1 tbsp olive oil
1 medium onion, peeled
   and finely sliced
400ml double cream
100ml whole milk
2 garlic cloves, peeled
   and finely chopped
30g butter, plus extra
   for greasing
500g turnips, peeled
   and finely sliced
500g potatoes (Maris
   Pipers are good), peeled
   and finely sliced
fine sea salt and
   white pepper

skin is dark brown – the fat will come out. Turn the breasts over, add the butter and continue cooking them for 2–3 minutes, basting them with the butter. Season well.

6 Strain the cherries, then put the liquid in a pan and reduce over a medium heat until it's thick and syrupy. Put the cherries back in this sauce and serve with the duck and the gratin.

STUFFED FOUR-BIRD ROAST

This is the most wonderful way to serve a turkey at Christmas. Ask your butcher to bone the birds for you, but make sure they leave the bones in the turkey drumsticks and outer wings. These will help to make the reconstructed bird look like a turkey again. You need a trussing needle and some butchers' string.

SERVES 12 AT LEAST

1 x 5kg turkey, boned but
    with drumsticks and
    outer wing bones intact
2 boneless duck
    breasts, skinned
2 boneless pheasant
    breasts, skinned
2 boneless guinea fowl
    breasts and 2 boneless
    thighs, skinned
fine sea salt and
    black pepper

Stuffing 1
30g butter
1 onion, peeled and
    finely chopped
1 Cox apple, peeled, cored
    and finely chopped
1 tsp golden caster sugar
25g chopped hazelnuts
100g fresh white
    breadcrumbs
5 fresh sage leaves,
    chopped
1 tbsp chopped
    curly parsley

Continued...

1 For the first stuffing, melt the butter in a pan, add the onion and apple and soften them over a gentle heat without browning. Sprinkle in the sugar and cook for a couple of minutes, then add the nuts and cook for 2 more minutes. Tip the mixture into a bowl and mix in the breadcrumbs and herbs. Season well. For the second stuffing, mix all the ingredients together in a bowl. Season well.

2 Lay the boned turkey out on a flat surface, skin side down, and season it with salt and pepper. Spread over some of the first stuffing, then put a duck breast on each side. Add some of the second stuffing to fill the spaces and make the surface smooth. Add the remaining meats in the same way, alternating the stuffings and seasoning each layer.

3 Now pull the sides of the turkey together (like a cardigan) – another pair of hands is invaluable here. Tuck in the edges and, using a trussing needle and butchers' string, stitch the turkey together very securely, starting at the neck end. Turn the bird over so the stitched side is underneath. Now take a really long piece of string – about 3 metres. Start by knotting the crossed drumsticks together using the mid-section of the string. Then criss-cross the strings underneath the bird and take them round the back, pulling the drumsticks in to make a neater shape. Criss-cross them again and take them back round the wings to the neck end, pulling the wings into the sides, and tie securely. You could also tie another piece of string around the bird to hold it together. Preheat the oven to 190°C/Fan 170°C/Gas 5.

4 Weigh the bird and work out the cooking time – it will need about 40 minutes per kilogram. Place it in a roasting tin, then roast it for the required time.

Stuffing 2
600g sausage meat
2 medium onions, peeled
   and finely chopped
3 tbsp dried cranberries
3 tbsp chopped
   curly parsley
1 egg, beaten

Fifteen minutes before the end of the cooking time, turn the heat up to 220°C/Fan 200°C/Gas 7 to brown the skin. Remove the turkey from the oven, put it on a board and cover with a double layer of foil. Leave it to rest for 1 hour.

5 Remove the string. Cut the turkey down the middle with a serrated knife. Taking one half at a time, turn it cut side down and carve it across into slices. Each slice will contain a mixture of meats and stuffing.

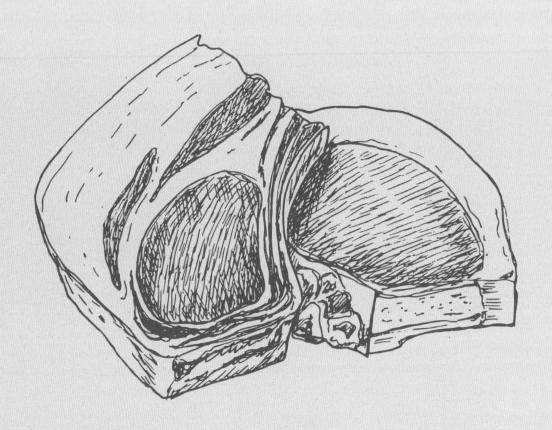

MEAT

*The chapter begins with the basics, then progresses, skill by skill,
recipe by recipe, up to showpiece dishes that really wow.*

MEAT IS AN EXCELLENT SOURCE OF PROTEIN, rich in B vitamins and iron. I enjoy eating meat, but not every day, and I like to bulk it out with plenty of vegetables. You don't always have to pay a fortune for meat. I find that some of the cheaper cuts are the tastiest – you just have to spend a bit more time and care when cooking them. In this chapter I have included recipes for beef, lamb and pork and also for venison, which is a great favourite of mine and well worth trying.

Buy your meat carefully and get the best you can afford. Look for beautiful pink meat with a nice marbling of fat – the creamier the fat the better. Creamy-coloured fat shows that the meat has been reared properly, while white fat is a sign of intensively reared animals.

I do like to buy my meat from a butcher whenever possible. Butchers' meat is properly hung – hanging helps to tenderise meat and allows it to develop flavour. Your butcher should be able to advise you on the best cuts for your dish and how to prepare meat.

Some supermarkets, though, are now making an effort to bring produce from local farmers into their shops and selling meat from named breeds. This is in response to people taking a greater interest in where their meat comes from and how the animals are reared.

STORING MEAT
Store meat at the bottom of the fridge, so it can't drip on any other foods, and cover it carefully. If you've bought meat that's wrapped in plastic, unwrap it, so it can breathe, then dry it off and cover it. I usually wrap my meat in greaseproof paper and put it on a plate. You can keep meat for a couple of days, but usually no more than four.

PREPARING
Meat cooked on the bone can be tastier, but a boned joint is very convenient and simpler to carve and serve.

Never cook your meat straight from the fridge. Allow it come to room temperature first and it will cook more evenly.

RESTING MEAT
It really is vital to leave meat to rest after cooking. It allows some of the juices to be reabsorbed so they are more evenly distributed through the meat. This makes it more tender and much nicer to eat. Rest a joint of meat for a good 20–30 minutes or so and smaller pieces, such as steak and chops, for 10 minutes. Cover resting meat loosely – never wrap it tightly or it will sweat.

BEEF
Top-quality beef is worth every penny. The ideal is meat from grass-fed cattle that have spent most of their life outdoors. The meat really does taste better. Try cheaper cuts too – they are delicious.

Cheek: This has excellent flavour, but it needs long slow cooking, so good for braises and casseroles.
Neck and clod: Both these are inexpensive cuts, good for long slow cooking. Often sold as stewing steak.

BEEF CUTS

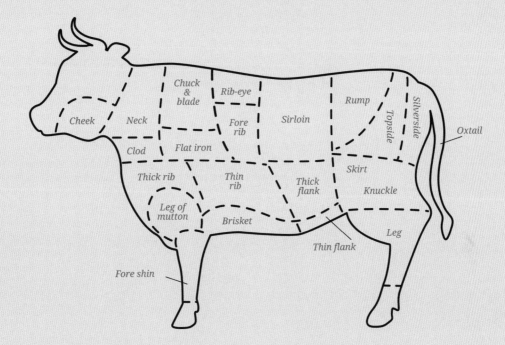

Chuck & blade • Rib-eye • Rump • Silverside • Cheek • Neck • Fore rib • Sirloin • Topside • Oxtail • Clod • Flat iron • Skirt • Thick rib • Thin rib • Thick flank • Knuckle • Leg of mutton • Brisket • Leg • Thin flank • Fore shin

Chuck and blade: Slightly more tender than neck and clod, these cuts are also good for braising and stews.

Rib-eye and flat iron: Both these are steak cuts, but rib-eye is more expensive and easier to cook. Flat iron is tasty but has to be cooked just right or it can be tough.

Fore rib and sirloin: These are excellent roasting cuts. Sirloin is costly but absolutely the best for a special occasion.

Rump: Cheaper than sirloin, rump is not quite as tender but has excellent flavour. Good for quick cooking, but it must be rested well.

Topside and silverside: A nice piece of topside from a good supplier can be roasted or braised and has good flavour. Silverside is great for pot roasts and traditionally used for salt beef.

Oxtail: Cheap and very delicious, oxtail must be cooked slowly and is ideal for stews, soups and rissoles.

Skirt: A cheap cut, this can be tough if overcooked.

Knuckle: This can be slow-cooked, roasted or cut into steaks. Knuckle steaks need careful cooking or they can be tough.

Thick flank: Also known as top rump, this can be braised or slow-roasted. Also good cut into strips for stir-fries.

Thin flank: Also known as hanger steak or onglet, this meat has plenty of marbling so very tasty.

Thin rib: Good for braising.

Brisket: Good for slow- roasting and pot-roasts; also used for making corned beef.

Thick rib: More tender than stewing steak, this is often used as braising steak.

Leg and fore-shin: Often used as stewing steak, both need long slow cooking.

Leg of mutton cut: Excellent for roasting (see page 206), this cut is much cheaper than sirloin. Ideally the sinew that runs through the meat should be removed.

LAMB CUTS

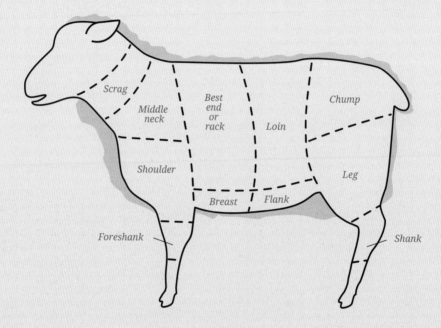

Scrag

Middle
neck

Best
end
or
rack

Loin

Chump

Shoulder

Leg

Breast   Flank

Foreshank

Shank

LAMB

Lamb is my favourite red meat. I love it and it is one of my staples in the kitchen. Spring lamb is delicious, but I also enjoy cooking hogget, which comes from animals more than one year old, and mutton, from two-year-old animals. Both have a stronger flavour than lamb. Sheep have to spend most of their life outside on grass and what they eat affects the flavour of the meat. I love salt-marsh lamb, and lamb from Scotland that have fed on heather.

Scrag: Cheap but tasty, this is excellent for slow-cooked stews and soups.
Middle neck: This is a tasty cut and is good braised on the bone.
Shoulder: Cheaper than leg and with great flavour, shoulder is good for roasting, particularly when slow-roasted. It can also be diced for use in stews and Scotch broth.

Best end or rack: A rack usually contains 8 ribs with very tender meat. It can be cooked quickly and is delicious but pricey.
Loin: This is very tender meat and a good roasting cut. Loin chops can be grilled or barbecued.
Chump: Good for chops or steaks.
Leg: Great for roasting, leg is leaner than shoulder but more expensive. It can be cooked pink.
Shank: Cheaper than leg, shanks have an excellent flavour. Good cooked very slowly on the bone.
Flank: This is fatty but very tasty and good for soup and stew. Flank is usually sold boned.
Breast: A very fatty cut but gorgeous when cooked very slowly. You can buy it on the bone, or boned and rolled.
Foreshank: This is from the lower part of the front leg and slightly smaller than shanks. Also good slow-cooked.

PORK CUTS

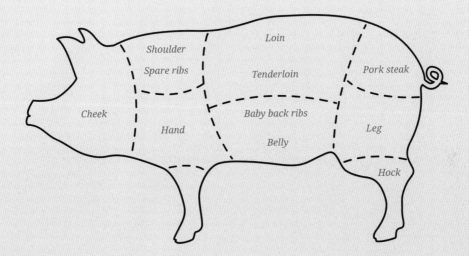

Shoulder
Spare ribs
Loin
Tenderloin
Pork steak
Cheek
Hand
Baby back ribs
Belly
Leg
Hock

PORK

The pig is the most versatile animal and you can eat almost every part of it. I've concentrated on the most generally used cuts, but people also eat trotters and ears, and pig's head terrine is now a fashionable dish. I do prefer to avoid buying meat from factory-farmed animals, which can be bland and tends to look white and damp. If possible, go for free-range pork and choose meat that is firm and pink.

Cheek: Very cheap but delicious, cheeks become meltingly tender when slow-cooked. Also good for mincing.

Shoulder: Excellent slow-roasted on or off the bone. Try my recipe for pulled pork on page 184. Shoulder is also good diced or minced for use in curries and Thai dishes.

Spare ribs: These have sweet, tasty meat and are ideal cooked on a barbecue.

Loin: This has quite lean meat and is a classic roasting cut, on or off the bone. Keep the skin on for good crackling.

Tenderloin: A very useful lean cut, this is delicious stuffed, rolled and steamed, then finished off in a pan.

Pork steak: Lovely lean meat that can be braised, grilled or barbecued.

Leg: This can be roasted but it is low in fat so not good for slow-roasting. Also used for pork escalopes, which can be cooked quickly.

Hock: This has a great flavour but must be cooked slowly. Good braised or pot-roasted.

Baby back ribs: These are just right for barbecue dishes and Chinese-style ribs. Try my recipe on page 191.

Belly: Cheap and tasty, belly must be slow-cooked. It is high in fat but has loads of flavour.

Hand: This is good slow-roasted or braised and is also used for pork mince.

SPICED APPLE TEA
ROLLED PORK FILLET

This is an unusual dish and I think the tea adds a lovely flavour to the meat.
You can experiment with different teas, but make sure the ingredients go
well with the pork. Good served with Peas à la Française (see page 99).

SERVES 4

2 pork fillets, about
    400g each, trimmed
4 camomile and spiced
    apple tea bags
1 tbsp vegetable oil
50g butter
2 garlic cloves, peeled
    and crushed
2 thyme sprigs
fine sea salt

1 Take the pork out of the fridge an hour or so before
you want to cook so it is at room temperature. This
will help it cook more evenly. Open the tea bags and
empty the contents on to a plate. Season the pork
fillets with salt on all sides, then roll them in the
tea-bag mixture.

2 Preheat the oven to 180°C/Fan 160°C/Gas 4. Heat
the vegetable oil in a ovenproof frying pan over a
medium heat – you don't want the pan too hot or
the tea will burn and the meat will dry out. Place the
tea-coated pork fillets in the pan and seal them on all
sides until light golden brown. Add the butter, garlic
and thyme, then baste the pork with the flavoured
butter, using a metal spoon. Put the pan in the oven
for 12–15 minutes.

3 Place a digital meat thermometer into the thickest
part of the pork and check that a temperature of 58°C
has been reached. This will ensure that the meat is
cooked while remaining nice and moist. If the meat
hasn't reached this temperature, put it back in the
oven for a few more minutes.

4 When the meat is done, place it on a rack over a plate
and pour over the juices from the pan. Leave it to rest
for at least 10 minutes before serving.

♀ COOK'S TIP ♀
I also like to use lemon verbena or blackcurrant
and rhubarb tea for this recipe.

PULLED PORK SHOULDER
WITH CIDER

I adore pulled pork and I love the way the meat becomes so meltingly tender that you can just pull it apart with a couple of forks. The cider goes wonderfully well with it. This is great served just as it is or packed into rolls.

SERVES 6

vegetable oil, for greasing
1 x 2kg boned pork
   shoulder
1 tbsp dried chilli flakes
1 tbsp wholegrain
   mustard
200ml white wine vinegar
250ml cider
3 onions, peeled and
   finely sliced
6 garlic cloves, peeled
   and sliced
fine sea salt and
   black pepper

1 Preheat the oven to 180°C/Fan 160°C/Gas 4. Oil a roasting tin and add the pork shoulder. Mix the chilli flakes and mustard with some salt and black pepper, then rub this mixture into the pork shoulder.

2 Pour over the vinegar and cider, then scatter the onions and garlic over the meat. Cover the pork with baking paper, then wrap it in foil.

3 Roast the pork in the preheated oven for 30 minutes, then turn the temperature down to 160°C/Fan 140°C/Gas 3 and roast for another 2½ hours. Remove the baking paper and foil, then roast for another 30 minutes.

4 The pork should be falling apart so you can just stick in a fork and 'pull' it apart with another fork.

FLAT IRON STEAK

Flat iron is cheaper than some types of steak but no less tasty. Because cheaper cuts of meat are usually from working muscle, it's even more important to make sure they are rested properly, giving the muscle time to relax and become tender. This is not a steak you can serve well done – if you overcook flat iron it will be tough. These are large steaks, so you could serve one between two people.

SERVES 2

2 x 225g flat iron steaks
2 tbsp vegetable oil
50g butter
2 garlic cloves, peeled
   and crushed
1 thyme sprig
fine sea salt

Marinade
2 garlic cloves, peeled
   and finely chopped
4 tbsp olive oil
2 tbsp red wine vinegar
2 tbsp finely chopped
   thyme
zest of ½ lemon
good grinding of
   black pepper

1 Put all the marinade ingredients into a sealable food bag. Add the steaks and leave them to marinate in the fridge for at least 4 hours or preferably overnight. Remove the steaks from the fridge at least 2 hours before cooking so they can come up to room temperature. This helps them cook more evenly.

2 Remove the steaks from the marinade and pat them dry with kitchen paper.

3 Heat the vegetable oil in a frying pan over a high heat. Season the steaks with salt on both sides, place them in the pan and seal for 2 minutes on one side and 1 minute on the other side until golden brown. Turn the heat down to medium and add the butter, garlic and thyme. Using a metal spoon, baste the steaks with the flavoured butter, then insert a digital meat thermometer into the thickest part of the steak. Cook and baste the steaks until your desired temperature is reached.

4 Place the steaks on a wire rack over a plate and pour over the contents of the pan. Leave them to rest for at least 10 minutes before serving.

Steak temperatures
Rare: 45–50°C; **Medium rare:** 54–56°C;
Medium: 60–62°C.

RIB-EYE STEAK WITH CHIMICHURRI SAUCE

Rib-eye steaks have a lovely marbling of fat, which makes them particularly tasty and succulent – they are my favourite. These are big steaks and one could be shared between two people, but I think that big steaks cook better. They go beautifully with a spoonful or two of chimichurri, a delicious South American herb sauce.

SERVES 2

2 x 250g rib-eye steaks
2 tbsp vegetable oil
50g butter
2 garlic cloves, peeled and finely chopped
1 thyme sprig
fine sea salt

Chimichurri sauce
2 long fresh red chillies, seeded and finely chopped
3 garlic cloves, peeled and finely chopped
2 large handfuls of curly parsley, leaves only, chopped
4 heaped tsp dried oregano
2 tsp flaked sea salt
5 tbsp red wine vinegar
5 tbsp extra virgin olive oil

1   Take the steaks out of the fridge at least 2 hours before cooking so they can come up to room temperature. This will help them cook more evenly

2   To make the chimichurri sauce, put the chopped chillies in a bowl with the rest of the ingredients and add 5 tablespoons of cold water. Stir until everything is well combined, then set aside.

3   Heat the vegetable oil in a frying pan over a high heat. Season the steaks with salt on both sides, place them in the pan and seal for 2 minutes on one side and 1 minute on the other side until golden brown. Turn the heat down to medium and add the butter, garlic and thyme. Using a metal spoon, baste the steaks with the flavoured butter, then insert a digital meat thermometer into the thickest part of the steak. Cook and baste until your desired temperature is reached.

4   Place the cooked steaks on a wire rack over a plate and pour over the contents of the pan. Leave the steaks to rest for at least 10 minutes before serving. Serve the steaks with a few spoonfuls of the chimichurri sauce.

Steak temperatures
Rare: 45–50°C; **Medium rare:** 54–56°C;
Medium: 60–62°C; **Medium well done:** 68–70°C;
Well done: 75–78°C.

LAMB BURGERS WITH MINT-PICKLED RED ONION AND CUMIN MAYONNAISE

I love lamb, so I sometimes like to make these as an alternative to regular beef burgers. I like my lamb just pink, not too rare, but adjust the cooking time to suit your taste. You can also cook these on a barbecue. Delicious served with the pickled onion slices and spicy mayonnaise.

SERVES 4

Burgers
3 tbsp vegetable oil
20g butter
2 banana shallots,
    peeled and diced
2 garlic cloves, peeled
    and crushed
4 tsp ground cumin
650g lamb mince
handful of coriander,
    chopped
1 egg yolk
fine sea salt

Mint-pickled red onion
1 red onion, peeled
    and finely sliced
150ml white wine vinegar
150g golden caster sugar
2 mint sprigs
juice and zest of 1 lime

Cumin mayonnaise
2 tsp cumin seeds
2 egg yolks
juice of 1 lime
100ml olive oil
200ml vegetable oil

To serve
4 burger buns
lettuce leaves

1 For the mint-pickled onion, put the slices of onion in a heatproof bowl. Put the vinegar, sugar, mint, lime juice and zest into a pan, add 250ml of water and bring it to the boil. Pour the liquid over the onion in the bowl, then set it aside to cool. This keeps in the fridge for at least 3 weeks and improves with age.

2 For the mayonnaise, put the cumin seeds in a small dry frying pan and cook them over a medium heat for a minute until you smell their aroma. Tip them into a spice grinder and grind them to form a powder.

3 Put the egg yolks in a large bowl and add the ground cumin seeds and the lime juice. Using an electric hand mixer, whisk the ingredients until they are well combined. While continuing to whisk, slowly start adding the olive oil, a little at a time. If you pour too fast or add too much oil in one go, the mayonnaise will split. Then do the same with the vegetable oil to make a thick glossy mayonnaise. If the mayo gets too thick, whisk in a tablespoon of cold water to thin it down. Check for seasoning and add salt if needed. Store the mayonnaise in the fridge for up to 4 days.

4 Now make the burgers. Place a small pan over a medium heat, then add a tablespoon of the oil and the butter. Allow the butter to melt, then turn the heat down low and add the shallots. Cook them for about 2 minutes until soft and translucent, then add the garlic and cumin and cook for a further minute. Remove the pan from the heat and leave to cool.

5 Put the lamb mince in a large bowl and add the cooled shallot mixture, then the chopped coriander, egg yolk and a teaspoon of salt. Mix the ingredients

together with your hands until well combined, then divide it into 4 evenly sized balls. Flatten each ball into a burger about 1cm thick. Leave the burgers to rest in the fridge for at least 30 minutes.

6   Heat the remaining oil in a frying pan over a medium-high heat. When the oil is hot, add the burgers to the pan and cook them on one side for about 4 minutes until golden brown. Turn them over and cook on the other side for another 3–4 minutes, then check they are done to your liking.

7   Serve the burgers in buns with some drained pickled red onion, lettuce leaves and cumin mayonnaise.

SLOW-ROAST SHOULDER OF LAMB WITH PRESERVED LEMONS

To my mind, this is one of the best ways to cook lamb – it's really easy and results in meltingly tender meat. I like to serve this with salad and Garlic and Sesame Seed Potato Wedges (see page 90). The Red Pepper Sauce (see page 276) also goes well.

SERVES 6

1 x 2.5kg shoulder
    of lamb, boned
2 preserved lemons,
    pulp removed
1 heaped tsp ground
    coriander
1 tsp ground cinnamon
4 tbsp olive oil
4 garlic cloves, peeled
    and crushed
4 thyme sprigs, chopped
handful of chopped
    parsley
1 Spanish onion, peeled
    and finely sliced
2 cinnamon sticks
1 tbsp runny honey
fine sea salt and
    black pepper

1 Preheat the oven to 200°C/Fan 180°C/Gas 6. Lay the boned lamb, skin side down, on a board and season it with salt and pepper. Cut one of the preserved lemon skins into strips. Mix the ground spices with the olive oil, garlic, lemon strips, thyme and parsley, then rub the mixture into the lamb flesh thoroughly.

2 Roll up the shoulder, skin side out, and tie it tightly with butchers' string in about 8 places.

3 Put the sliced onion and the cinnamon sticks in a roasting tin and lay the lamb on top. Rub the runny honey into the skin, then completely cover the lamb with foil. Roast the lamb in the preheated oven for 30 minutes, then turn the temperature down to 150°C/Fan 130°C/Gas 2 and cook for another 3 hours.

4 Remove the lamb from the oven, take off the foil and put the lamb back in the oven for another 15 minutes. Remove, then leave the lamb to rest for 20 minutes.

5 The meat should be falling apart so it's no trouble to carve. Serve the lamb with the other preserved lemon cut into thin strips.

♈ COOK'S TIP ♈

If you don't have any preserved lemons, thinly pare the peel of a fresh lemon and cut it into strips. Put the strips in a pan with 2 tablespoons of water, a dessert spoon of sea salt and a knob of butter and cook for 2 minutes, then drain.

BARBECUE BABY BACK PORK RIBS

Serve these for a summer barbecue with lots of salads and
everyone will be happy. They do have to be marinated and
then cooked for a long time, but you can do most of the work
well in advance and finish them off at the last minute.

SERVES 4

1 tbsp vegetable oil
1 small white onion,
   peeled and chopped
3 garlic cloves, peeled
   and crushed
1 fresh red chilli,
   finely chopped
1 tsp fennel seeds,
   crushed
55g dark soft brown sugar
50ml dark soy sauce
300ml tomato ketchup
2 whole baby back ribs
200ml cider
fine sea salt and
   black pepper

1 Heat the vegetable oil in a pan over a medium
   heat, then cook the onion for 2 minutes. Add the
   garlic, chilli and fennel seeds and cook for a further
   2 minutes. Add the sugar and cook for another
   minute, then add the soy sauce and ketchup and
   season with salt and pepper. Bring the mixture to
   the boil, then turn down the heat and simmer for
   3 minutes to combine the flavours.

2 Put the baby back ribs in a baking tin and coat them
   with the sauce. Cover and leave them in the fridge
   to marinate for up to 24 hours – the longer they
   marinate, the better the flavour.

3 Preheat the oven to 160°C/Fan 140°C/Gas 3. Pour the
   cider into the tin around the ribs. Cover the tin with
   foil and cook the ribs for 3 hours or until the meat is
   tender, turning them every 30 minutes or so. If you
   like, you can prepare the ribs to this point the day
   before.

4 Remove the foil and put the tin back in the oven for
   20–25 minutes, checking the ribs every 5 minutes
   until they are nice and sticky. The ribs are now ready
   to eat or you could put them on a barbecue for a few
   minutes for a smokier flavour.

MEAT

LASAGNE

Sadly we've all got used to somewhat sub-standard lasagne served up in pubs, but when properly made at home this is a really splendid dish and a great family favourite. It does take a little while to put together but it's so well worth it. And it can all be prepared the day before, ready to pop into the oven when you want it, so is perfect for entertaining.

SERVES 4

7–8 dried lasagne
   sheets (about 130g)
75g Cheddar cheese,
   grated

Bolognese sauce
1 tbsp vegetable oil
4 rashers of smoked
   streaky bacon,
   finely diced
700g beef mince
1 medium white onion,
   peeled and finely diced
1 celery stick, finely diced
2 medium carrots, peeled
   and finely diced
2 garlic cloves, peeled
   and finely chopped
leaves from 2 rosemary
   sprigs, finely chopped
3 tbsp tomato purée
1 tsp dried oregano
200ml red wine
250g ripe fresh tomatoes,
   roughly chopped
350ml beef stock
2 bay leaves
handful of fresh basil
fine sea salt and
   black pepper

Continued...

1 Start by making the Bolognese sauce. Heat the oil in a large heavy-based pan over a medium heat. Gently fry the bacon until golden and crisp, then add the mince to the pan and cook until browned all over.

2 Add the onion, celery, carrots, garlic and rosemary to the pan and gently fry for 8–10 minutes until everything has softened. Stir in the tomato purée and oregano and cook for 2–3 minutes, then add the wine, bring to the boil and continue to cook until the wine has reduced by half.

3 Stir in the chopped tomatoes, beef stock and bay leaves, then bring to a gentle simmer. Reduce the heat, put a lid on the pan and leave the sauce to simmer for about an hour until the flavours have developed. Stir occasionally to make sure it doesn't catch on the base of the pan. Season with salt and pepper and finish with the basil.

4 For the béchamel, pour the milk into a pan and add the parsley stalks, bay leaves and peppercorns. Place the pan over a low heat and slowly bring the milk to simmering point. Remove the pan from the heat and set it aside to allow the flavours to infuse.

5 Gently melt the butter in a separate pan without allowing it to colour. Turn the heat up to medium and stir in the flour, mixing vigorously to make a smooth paste. Remove the pan from the heat, then pour in the infused milk, a little at a time, through a sieve, whisking it into the flour and butter paste.

6 Place the pan back over a low heat and cook the béchamel sauce for 5 minutes, whisking from time to time to keep it smooth. Add salt to taste.

Béchamel sauce
900ml whole milk
2 parsley stalks
2 bay leaves
12 black peppercorns
120g butter
80g plain flour

7   Take a deep ovenproof dish, measuring about
    22 x 26cm, and spoon in a third of the meat sauce.
    Spread it out evenly. Cover this with a thin layer of
    the béchamel sauce, then a layer of pasta sheets,
    taking care not to overlap them.

8   Repeat these layers twice more, finishing with a
    layer of béchamel and top with the grated Cheddar.
    Set the lasagne aside for an hour to settle.

9   Preheat the oven to 200°C/Fan 180°C/Gas 6 and cook
    the lasagne for 35–40 minutes or until golden brown
    and bubbling round the edges. To check, insert
    a knife into the centre. If it cuts through without
    resistance, the lasagne is ready.

STIR-FRIED BEEF GOULASH

This is a quick way of making a goulash and perfect when you want something good, hearty and delicious in a hurry. The trick is not to overcook the steak – you want to keep it tender and succulent.

SERVES 4

olive oil, for frying
600g rump steak, cut
    into thin strips
5 rashers of smoked
    streaky bacon,
    cut into strips
3 red peppers
300g red onions,
    peeled and sliced
2 garlic cloves, peeled
    and chopped
1 heaped tbsp sweet
    smoked paprika
1 tsp ground mixed spice
8 cardamom seeds
    (the tiny black ones
    inside pod), ground
1 tsp chilli powder
400g can of tomatoes
200ml beef stock
handful of finely chopped
    parsley, to garnish
150ml soured cream,
    to serve
fine sea salt and
    black pepper

1 Heat a drizzle of oil in a large frying pan over a high heat. Brown the steak, a batch at a time, on all sides, setting each batch aside as it is ready and adding more oil if needed. It's important not to overcrowd the pan or the meat will steam and not brown.

2 Once all the beef is done, brown the bacon in the pan and set it aside with the beef.

3 Cut the red peppers into quarters, remove the seeds and white pith, then cut the peppers across into slices. Add the peppers and onions to the pan and brown them over a medium heat, then stir in the garlic, paprika, mixed spice, cardamom seeds and chilli powder and cook for 3 minutes. Roughly chop the tomatoes and add them with the beef stock. Bring to a simmer and cook for another 5 minutes, then season with salt and pepper.

4 Put the cooked beef and bacon back in the pan, gently fold them into the other ingredients and cook for another couple of minutes. Taste and add more seasoning if needed.

5 Sprinkle with parsley and serve with soured cream. Some plain basmati rice is good with this.

RICH LAMB NECK CASSEROLE

This is my take on Lancashire hot pot, using lovely best end of neck chops. Everything is cooked in one pot, so it is simple to do and really delicious. All you need are some green vegetables on the side.

SERVES 4

4 rashers of smoked
   streaky bacon, chopped
150g plain flour,
   for dusting
6 best end of neck lamb
   chops, about 2cm thick
1 tbsp olive oil
100ml wine (or
   extra stock)
2 tsp runny honey
1 Spanish onion,
   peeled and sliced
4 bay leaves
1 tsp dried thyme
2 garlic cloves
400g can of flageolet
   beans, drained
500ml chicken stock
500g potatoes (such
   as Maris Pipers),
   peeled and sliced
fine sea salt and
   black pepper

1 In a large frying pan, brown the bacon, then set it aside. Put the flour in a bowl and season it with salt and pepper, then dust the lamb chops with the flour. Shake off any excess. Heat the oil in the frying pan, add the chops and brown them over a medium heat on both sides. Set them aside.

2 Now deglaze the pan – pour in the wine (or extra stock) and let it sizzle, scraping up any sticky bits. Stir in the honey, then set the pan and juices aside. Preheat the oven to 180°C/Fan 160°C/Gas 4.

3 Now assemble the casserole. Add half the bacon, onion, herbs, garlic, beans and stock to a large casserole dish. Put the lamb chops on top, add the rest of the bacon, onion, herbs, garlic and beans. Layer the slices of potato on top, then pour on the juices from the frying pan and the rest of the stock.

4 Cover the dish with a tight-fitting lid and cook in the preheated oven for 2 hours. For a crispier top, remove the lid and cook for a further 30 minutes. Serve with some greens.

TRADITIONAL STEAK AND KIDNEY PIE

One of the best of all British dishes, a really good steak and
kidney pie is a wonder to behold. If you're one of those people
who don't like kidney, don't worry – just leave it out and add
more steak. Your pie will still be utterly delicious.

SERVES 4

300g ox kidney
50g plain flour, plus
    extra for dusting
900g chuck steak,
    trimmed and cut
    into 3cm cubes
2 tbsp olive oil
60g butter
1 large onion, finely sliced
2 garlic cloves, crushed
200g button mushrooms
1 tbsp chopped thyme
800ml good beef stock
2 tsp Worcestershire
    sauce
1 x 400g packet of
    puff pastry
1 egg, beaten
fine sea salt and
    black pepper

1 Preheat the oven to 200°C/Fan 180°C/Gas 6. First
prepare the kidney. Slice the kidney in half to expose
the tough white core inside. Remove this core by
cutting around it with a sharp knife, then cut the
kidney into large pieces. Put the flour in a large bowl
and season it with salt and plenty of black pepper.
Add pieces of kidney and steak and toss to coat
them in the flour.

2 Heat the oil in a large, flameproof casserole dish
and brown the meat in batches over a medium heat.
Don't overcrowd the pan or the meat will steam
and not brown. Set the meat aside as it is browned.

3 Turn down the heat and add the butter, then
sauté the onion and garlic until softened. Add
the mushrooms and thyme and sauté for another
few minutes, then add any leftover flour, and cook
for a further minute. Pour in the stock and the
Worcestershire sauce.

4 Put the meat back in the dish and bring to the
boil. Cover the casserole dish with a lid, place it
in the middle of the preheated oven and cook for
30 minutes. Turn the temperature down to 170°C/
Fan 150°C/Gas 3½ and cook for another 1–1¼ hours,
until the meat is tender. Check for seasoning. Tip
everything into a deep pie dish, either an oval dish
about 26 x 19cm or a rectangular one with a similar
capacity. Leave the meat to cool. It's good to get all
this done the day before you want to serve the pie,
if possible.

5 Preheat the oven to 200°C/Fan 180°C/Gas 6. Roll out
the pastry on a floured work surface to a thickness
of about 3mm and about the same shape as your
pie dish. Cut a 2cm-wide ribbon from the pastry

and place this strip around the rim of the pie dish, pressing it down. Brush the rim of pastry with water. Trim the rest of the pastry to about 2.5cm bigger than the top of the pie dish. Sit a pie funnel in the centre of the filling to support the pastry.

6 Roll the pastry lid on to the rolling pin and place it over the filling. Trim off any excess pastry, then press the edges with a fork to seal it firmly. Brush the top of the pie with beaten egg and make a hole in the centre over the funnel. Bake for 35–40 minutes until the pastry is golden and crisp and the filling is hot.

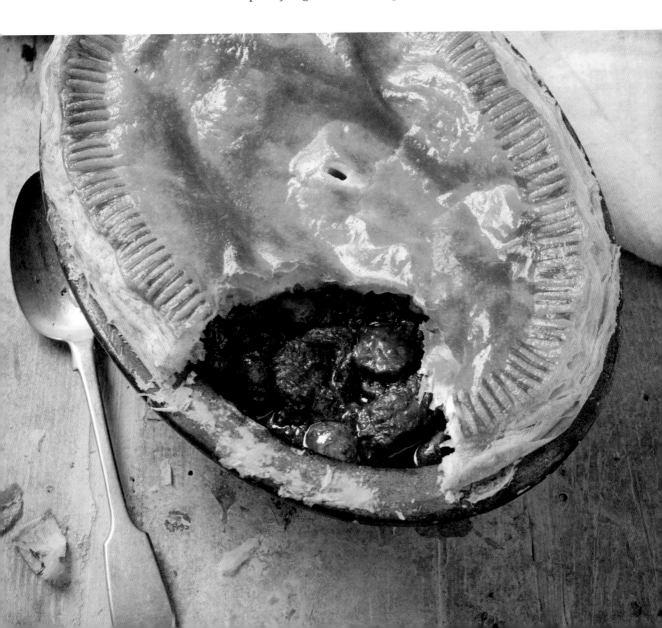

TRADITIONAL ROAST LEG OF LAMB

Lamb is perhaps my favourite roast but I don't like it rare. For me, slightly pink lamb is just right and that's what this recipe will give you. It makes a perfect Sunday lunch for the family.

SERVES 6

2 leeks, chopped into
    2.5cm chunks
2 white onions, peeled
    and quartered
3 carrots, peeled and cut
    into 2.5cm chunks
2 celery sticks, cut into
    2.5cm chunks
250ml white wine
2 garlic bulbs, cut in
    half crossways
1 x 2.5kg leg of lamb
fine sea salt and
    black pepper

Gravy
30g plain flour
300ml red wine
3 rosemary sprigs
500ml lamb stock

1 Scatter the leeks, onions, carrots and celery into a large roasting tin. Preheat the oven to 180°C/Fan 160°C/Gas 4.

2 Season the lamb with salt and pepper and lay it on top of the vegetables in the roasting tin, then pour in the white wine.

3 Put the lamb in the oven and roast for 1½ hours, adding the garlic halfway through the cooking time. Check the meat with a digital thermometer. It should be 51–54°C for medium rare, 57–60°C for medium (still pink), and 68–70°C for well done. Remove the meat from the oven, place it on a rack and leave it to rest for at least 20 minutes before carving.

4 For the gravy, carefully pour the excess fat from the roasting tin into a bowl, leaving about a tablespoon behind. Place the tin over a medium heat, stir in the flour and cook for 2 minutes, stirring continuously. Add the wine and keep stirring to stop the gravy going lumpy. Add the rosemary and continue to cook until the wine has reduced by half. Add the lamb stock, bring to the boil, then strain the gravy through a fine sieve into a pan. Press it through well to extract all the flavours from the veg. Bring back to the boil, then reduce the heat and simmer until the gravy begins to thicken. Season the gravy and pour it into a sauce boat or jug.

5 Serve the lamb with the gravy and perhaps some Dauphinoise Potatoes (see page 105) and cabbage.

BRAISED OXTAIL AND BUTTERY MASH

A quintessentially British dish, braised oxtail is a real winter warmer.
Oxtail is a cheap cut, so you get a lot for your money, and as long as it
is cooked for a good long time, it makes a wonderfully tasty meal.

SERVES 4

plain flour, for dusting
2kg oxtail, trimmed of fat
3 tbsp rapeseed oil
4 rashers of smoked
   streaky bacon, diced
2 medium onions, peeled
   and quartered
2 medium carrots, peeled
   and cut into chunks
2 celery sticks, chopped
2 tbsp red wine vinegar
700ml red wine or
   extra stock
1 litre beef stock
2 tbsp tomato purée
4 thyme sprigs
3 bay leaves
a few strips of orange peel
3 tbsp redcurrant jelly
fine sea salt and
   black pepper

Buttery mash
1kg floury potatoes (such
   as King Edwards),
   peeled and quartered
150g butter
4 tbsp finely snipped
   chives
fine sea salt and
   white pepper

1 Season the flour with salt and pepper, then dust the pieces of oxtail with the flour. Preheat the oven to 210°C/Fan 190°C/Gas 6½.

2 Heat the oil in a large frying pan and brown the oxtail on all sides over a medium heat. Brown a batch at a time so you don't overcrowd the pan. Place the browned oxtail in a large casserole dish. Fry the bacon until golden brown, then add it to the dish.

3 Brown the onions, carrots and celery in the frying pan and add them to the casserole dish. Add the vinegar to the pan, letting it sizzle and scraping up any sticky bits, then add the red wine (or extra stock) and cook until reduced by half. Pour the contents of the pan into the dish and add the stock, purée, herbs and orange peel.

4 Put the casserole dish into the preheated oven and cook, uncovered, for 30 minutes. Check that the contents are simmering, then cover the dish, turn the heat down to 170°C/Fan 150°C/Gas 3½ and cook for another 3 hours.

5 When the oxtail is cooked, transfer it to a bowl with a slotted spoon. Strain the stock into another pan and reduce it on the hob until it thickens and makes a smooth sauce. Season well and stir in the redcurrant jelly, then put the oxtail back into the sauce and warm through if necessary. Serve with the buttery mash.

Buttery mash
1 Put the potatoes in a pan of cold water, add salt and bring to the boil. Cook the potatoes for about 20 minutes or until tender.

2 Drain, then tip the potatoes back in the pan. Add the butter and mash, then season and fold in the chives.

ROAST LOIN OF VENISON WITH BRAISED RED CABBAGE

This is a bit of a treat when venison is in season. The trick with venison loin is not to overcook it, as it is a very lean meat and can be dry if cooked for too long. Keep it rare and succulent for best results and always season it well before cooking. The cabbage is braised for a long time to make it really soft and delicious. Don't stint on the pepper – I think red cabbage should be good and peppery.

SERVES 4

1 x 1kg venison loin
2 tbsp vegetable oil
50g butter
2 garlic cloves, peeled
    and chopped
1 thyme sprig
fine sea salt

Braised red cabbage
100ml orange juice
100ml red wine
100ml red wine vinegar
150ml chicken stock
60g redcurrant jelly
2 liquorice sticks
    (optional)
2 cinnamon sticks
2 star anise
100g soft brown sugar
3 cloves
60g butter
1 small red cabbage,
    finely sliced
1 onion, peeled and
    finely sliced
fine sea salt and lots of
    black pepper (about 8
    turns of a pepper mill)

1 For the red cabbage, put all the ingredients except the butter, cabbage and onion in a pan, bring to a simmer. Take the pan off the heat and leave to infuse for at least 2 hours. For best results, leave the cooled liquid in the fridge overnight.

2 Melt half the butter in a large pan and gently cook the cabbage and onion. Strain the infused liquid through a fine sieve and pour it over the cabbage. Bring to the boil, then simmer over a low heat until the liquid has reduced and the cabbage is nicely glazed. This will take about 2 hours. Drain off the excess liquid, if there is any, then fold in the rest of the butter and season to taste with salt and lots of pepper.

3 Be sure to take the venison out of the fridge at least 2 hours before cooking, so it comes up to room temperature. Heat the oil in a large frying pan over a high heat. Season the meat with salt, add it to the pan and seal on all sides until golden brown. Turn the heat down to medium and add the butter, garlic and thyme. Baste the venison with the flavoured butter using a metal spoon. Insert a digital thermometer into the thickest part of the meat and cook until your desired temperature is reached – see below.

4 Place the meat on a wire rack over a plate and pour over the contents of the pan. Leave the meat to rest for at least 10 minutes, then serve with the cabbage.

Venison temperatures
Rare: 45–50°C; **Medium rare:** 54–56°C; **Medium:** 60–62°C; **Medium well done:** 68–70°C; **Well done:** 75–78°C.

VENISON CASSEROLE WITH PEPPERED DUMPLINGS

You can't beat a dumpling and I think this is a fabulous recipe. It's a spectacular dish to take to the table for everyone to admire.

SERVES 4–6

150g plain flour
1 x 1kg haunch of
    venison, boned and
    cut into 3cm cubes
60g butter
3 tbsp olive oil
5 rashers of smoked
    streaky bacon, cut
    into thin strips
1 medium onion, peeled
    and finely sliced
2 celery sticks,
    roughly chopped
200ml red wine
100ml port (optional)
1 tbsp golden caster sugar
game or chicken stock,
    to cover
2 garlic cloves, crushed
3 thyme sprigs
1 tbsp juniper berries,
    lightly crushed
1 bay leaf
fine sea salt and
    black pepper

Mushrooms
and shallots
10 shallots, peeled
    and left whole
2 tbsp olive oil
80g butter
10 button mushrooms
1 tbsp redcurrant jelly

Continued...

1 Put the flour in a bowl and season it with salt and pepper. Toss the venison in the flour to coat it well, then shake the meat to remove any excess. Preheat the oven to 180°C/Fan 160°C/Gas 4.

2 Heat half the butter and 2 tablespoons of the olive oil in a large frying pan and brown the venison over a medium heat. Brown the meat in batches, adding more butter as you need it, and remove each batch to a casserole dish once it is browned.

3 Using the same frying pan, add the remaining tablespoon of oil, and fry the bacon, then add it to the venison. Brown the onion and celery and add them to the casserole dish. Pour the wine and port, if using, into the frying pan to deglaze it. Boil for a couple of minutes, then tip it all into the casserole dish.

4 Add the sugar to the dish and pour in just enough stock to cover the venison, then add the garlic, thyme, juniper berries, bay leaf and a little seasoning. Place the lid on the dish and cook in the preheated oven for 2 hours, checking and stirring the meat halfway through the cooking time.

5 While the casserole is in the oven, you can cook the mushrooms and shallots. Bring a pan of water to simmering point, add the shallots and simmer them for 1 minute. Drain them well and set aside. Heat a tablespoon of the oil and half the butter in a frying pan and gently cook the mushrooms for 3–4 minutes until any liquid has evaporated and they are golden brown. Remove them from the pan and set aside. Add the remaining oil and the rest of the butter and sauté the shallots for 5 minutes until golden. Return the mushrooms to the pan with the shallots, season well, then mix in the redcurrant jelly. Set aside.

Dumplings
200g self-raising flour
100g vegetable suet
fine sea salt and
 black pepper

6 For the dumplings, sift the flour and a teaspoon
  of salt into a bowl and add plenty of black pepper.
  Stir in the suet, then add enough water to make soft,
  but not sticky, dough – you should need about 80ml.
  Roll the mixture into little balls of about 20g each.

7 When the venison is done, take the dish out of the
  oven. Add the mushrooms and shallots, then place
  the dumplings on top. Cover the dish and put it back
  in the oven for 10 minutes. Take the lid off and cook
  for another 10–15 minutes to brown the dumplings.

8 Serve the venison and dumplings with some green
  vegetables, such as French beans or cabbage.

BEEF BOURGUIGNON

This is a classic dish and is utterly delicious. It is hearty and robust, but with the little shallots and mushrooms it also looks very attractive and sophisticated when served, so is ideal for a meal with family or friends. I admit it's not the cheapest dish to make, as you need a whole bottle of wine – and I always think you need a decent wine for cooking, one you are happy to drink. Other than that, this is straightforward to cook and can be prepared ahead of time, which is always useful. Freezes like a dream too.

SERVES 6

2 heaped tbsp plain flour
1kg beef chuck, cut
    into 3cm chunks
vegetable oil, for frying
2 garlic cloves, peeled
    and thinly sliced
1 tbsp tomato purée
1 tbsp golden caster sugar
750ml bottle of red wine
    (Burgundy is good)
200ml beef stock
4 rashers of smoked
    streaky bacon, diced
150g small shallots, peeled
    but roots left intact
30g butter
250g button mushrooms
    (about 20 depending
    on size), cleaned
fine sea salt and
    white pepper

Bouquet garni
1 bay leaf
3 thyme sprigs
1 rosemary sprig
1 parsley stalk

1 Preheat the oven to 170°C/Fan 150°C/Gas 3½. Put the flour in a bowl, season it with salt and pepper, then toss the meat in the flour until lightly coated. Shake off any excess.

2 Place a large flameproof casserole dish over a medium-high heat and add a tablespoon of oil. Working in batches, so you don't overcrowd the pan, fry the meat on one side for about 3 minutes until golden brown, then turn it over and brown it on the other side. Set each batch aside while you brown the rest, adding more oil as necessary.

3 Add the garlic to the casserole dish and fry it until lightly browned, then put the meat and any juices back into the pan and stir in the tomato purée and sugar. Pour in the wine and the beef stock – the meat should bob up from the liquid and not be completely covered. Tie the ingredients for the bouquet garni together with string and add it to the pan, then bring to the boil, scraping up any caramelised cooking juices from the bottom of the pan. Place a lid on the casserole dish and cook for 1½ hours in the preheated oven.

4 Meanwhile, heat a little oil in a frying pan and fry the bacon until it is starting to crisp up. Set it aside, then add the shallots with 200ml of water and cook them until the water has evaporated. Add the butter and cook until the shallots are lightly coloured, then set them aside with the bacon. Put the button mushrooms into the frying pan with 100ml of water and cook until the water has evaporated. Put the bacon and shallots back into the pan and set them aside until the meat is nearly ready.

5 When the meat has cooked for 1½ hours, remove the dish from the oven and add the cooked bacon, shallots and mushrooms. Put the dish back in the oven and cook for another 30 minutes.

6 At the end of the cooking time, if the juices look watery, remove the meat, shallots and mushrooms with a slotted spoon and set them aside. Cook the juices over a high heat for a few minutes until they have thickened to a sauce consistency, then return the meat, shallots and mushrooms to the dish.

7 Season with salt and pepper and serve the beef with new potatoes smothered with lots of butter and chopped parsley.

MEAT

ROAST BEEF

I like to use the beef joint that butchers call 'leg of mutton' cut. You might not see it on the counter, but ask and they will get it for you. I find it really tasty, more tender than topside but not nearly as expensive as sirloin. If you can't get this joint, try good-quality topside instead. Serve the beef with just some roasted root vegetables or go the whole hog and do roast potatoes (see pages 88–9), Yorkshires (see page 30) and green vegetables.

SERVES 6

1 x 2kg 'leg of mutton' beef joint, sinew along the middle removed and the meat rolled and tied (ask your butcher to do this for you) 1 medium leek
1 medium onion, peeled and cut into eighths
2 carrots, peeled and cut into 1cm rounds
2 celery sticks, each cut into 3 pieces
4 garlic cloves, unpeeled
50g plain flour
1 heaped tbsp mustard powder
2 tbsp goose fat or lard, for sealing
fine sea salt and black pepper

Gravy
1 tbsp plain flour
200ml red wine (optional)
200ml good beef stock
1 tsp browning sauce
1 tbsp butter

1 Remove the meat from the fridge at least 45 minutes before cooking. Wash the leek and cut the white part and half the dark green leaves into large rounds – save the rest of the dark green leaves for another recipe. Place the leek with the rest of the vegetables and the garlic in a roasting tin to make a trivet for the beef. Preheat the oven to 200°C/Fan 180°C/Gas 6.

3 Mix the flour with the mustard in a bowl and season with salt and pepper. Dredge the beef in this mixture until the joint is completely covered. Heat the fat in a heavy-based pan until smoking hot, then sear the meat well on all sides and put it on top of the vegetables. Roast the beef in the preheated oven for 15 minutes per 500g, plus 10–15 minutes, until the internal temperature of the meat registers 50–55°C on a digital meat thermometer.

4 Take the meat out of the oven, put it on a rack over a plate to allow the juices to run and leave it to rest for at least 30 minutes before carving.

5 Meanwhile, make the gravy. There shouldn't be a lot of fat in the tin, but tip out any excess – you need to leave about a tablespoon. Sprinkle the flour on to the vegetables and mix well, then add the red wine and keep mixing and scraping up any sticky bits. Cook until the wine is reduced by half. Add the beef stock, browning sauce and any juices that have been released from the beef, then simmer for a few minutes. Season the gravy and strain it through a fine sieve into a small pan – press it through well to extract all the flavours from the veg. Bring to the boil, then add the butter and whisk until melted. Pour the gravy into a warm jug and serve it with the beef.

PUDDINGS & CAKES

The chapter begins with the basics, then progresses, skill by skill, recipe by recipe, up to showpiece dishes that really wow.

LIKE MANY PEOPLE, I DO LIKE TO FINISH A MEAL with a little something sweet. And there's something very civilised about a slice of cake or a biscuit or two with a cup of tea or coffee in the afternoon. I know these things are an indulgence, but once in a while they're fine – and if you are going to eat sweet things, home-made is best. Cakes and puddings are often the first dishes children learn to cook – I adore baking sessions with my grandchildren – but as adults many people get nervous about pastry-making and baking. In this chapter I want to guide you through making a range of desserts and cakes to suit every occasion.

PASTRY

Making pastry isn't difficult, but you do need to follow a few rules and get some practice. In the following chapter you'll find a good basic recipe for sweet shortcrust pastry that you can use for any sort of fruit tart, together with plenty of ideas for fillings. Master this pastry and you will always be able to come up with a delicious dessert. Yes, you can buy pastry but home-made is so much better and, as with bread, if you make it yourself you know exactly what's in it. Pastry freezes well too, so you can make a batch to stash in the freezer. I do, however, buy ready-made puff pastry, but I always go for an all-butter type.

Pastry can be made by hand or in a food processor. Don't overwork the pastry and be careful about adding the liquid – too little and the pastry will crack easily, but too much makes pastry difficult to work and tough. The more often you make pastry, the better you will be able to judge the liquid levels and get it just right. Pastry needs to be chilled before baking to rest the gluten. If you try to cook it straight away, the pastry will shrink too much.

When rolling out pastry, dust the work surface and the pastry generously so it doesn't stick. Use a good long rolling pin and never roll off the edge of the pastry – always stop just before it. Drape the pastry over the rolling pin to lift it and bring it to your tin.

Fruit tarts and pies are among my favourite desserts. I prefer to use fruit in season and choose whatever is best at the time. Look for fruit that's ripe but not too ripe and use plenty of it. One of my pet hates is a fruit pie with not enough fruit! When making apple pie, for example, I like to pile the slices of apple really high – see my recipe on page 224. It works, I promise you, and it is so delicious.

Avoid overcooking fruit for pies and tarts. I think it's best for the fruit to keep some texture, rather than let it cook down to a mush.

CAKES

I know you can buy a huge range of delicious cakes these days, but for me, nothing says love and family like a home-made cake. Even the simplest, such as my drizzle cake on page 237, is such a treat. In recent years baking has become hugely popular – thanks, in part, to certain television shows – and more people than ever are discovering the joys of making their own cakes and biscuits.

There are lots of different ways of making cakes, but the basic method starts by creaming the butter and sugar. Always use unsalted butter and make sure that the butter is at room temperature and soft before you start. Cream the butter and sugar with an electric hand mixer until the mixture is really fluffy, light and pale in colour. You will find that you need to keep going longer than you think for best results. One reason for cakes dipping in the middle is because the mixture has not been creamed for long enough.

When you add eggs to the butter and sugar, always add a little of the flour at the same time to stop the mixture from curdling. And use a metal spoon for mixing or folding ingredients together, as it cuts through the mixture more effectively than a wooden spoon or spatula – it's important to treat the mixture lightly so you don't knock out the air.

You do need to be exact when baking. With some types of dishes, such as soups, casseroles and salads, you can happily add a handful of this and that without worrying too much. But with baking you must get the balance exactly right. Get yourself a good set of scales and some measuring spoons and weigh and measure your ingredients carefully. Once you get more experienced, you can afford to experiment a bit more but when you're learning, follow the recipe.

CREAMY PUDDINGS
Crème caramel and crème brûlée are two of my very favourites. Retro they may be, but I think that these are really useful and gorgeous puddings, and they're made with ingredients that you can find anywhere. The brûlée topping has to be done at the last minute, but otherwise both of these can be made well in advance, so they're ideal when you're entertaining family and friends.

Always use double cream or whipping cream for puddings. When whipping cream, take care not to overwhip or it will start to separate. Just whip until the cream thickens, comes together and looks firm and opaque.

CHOCOLATE
I do love chocolate cake, mousse – everything made with chocolate. I always use good dark chocolate that contains 64–75% cocoa solids for making cakes and puddings. When melting chocolate, the secret is to be patient and don't rush. Break the chocolate up and put it in a heatproof bowl over a pan of simmering water. Don't allow the bottom of the bowl to touch the water or the chocolate will get too hot too quickly and go grainy. Leave it to melt slowly, then remove the pan from the heat. Allow the chocolate to cool slightly before adding it to other ingredients.

♟ COOK'S TIP ♟
Always make sure you line your cake tin properly, so that you can remove the cake easily and neatly without damaging the sides. The best way is to grease the tin lightly with oil or butter, then line the sides and base with baking paper – greasing first helps to keep the paper in place.

SPICED ROASTED PINEAPPLE

There are loads of lovely flavours here to bring out the best from
a sweet pineapple. This makes a excellent dessert with some
crème fraîche or you could also serve it with gammon.

SERVES 4

1 pineapple
2 tbsp Bacardi or
    Malibu (optional)
250ml pineapple juice
100g golden caster sugar
1 lemon grass
    stick, bashed
1 lime leaf
1 vanilla pod, split in half
1 star anise
½ cinnamon stick
50g butter, diced

1 Preheat the oven to 180°C/Fan 160°C/Gas 4. Peel
the pineapple, cut it into quarters lengthways and
remove the core. Brown the pieces of pineapple
gently in a hot dry frying pan, then add the Bacardi,
Malibu or 2 tablespoons of the pineapple juice. Stir to
deglaze the pan, scraping up any sticky bits. Tip the
contents of the pan into a roasting tin.

2 Put all the remaining ingredients into a pan and
bring to the boil, then pour everything into the
roasting tin with the pineapple. Roast the pineapple
for 40–50 minutes until soft, then leave it to cool.

3 Pour the liquid into a pan and cook until reduced and
syrupy. Ideally, check this with a thermometer and
don't let it heat to more than 100–110°C. Set the syrup
aside to cool, then serve it with the roasted pineapple.
Serve with some crème fraîche if you like.

213

LEMON POSSET

Simple yet sophisticated, this is a great standby pudding that you can make at any time of year. There are only three ingredients and you can prepare it in minutes, then leave it to chill until you're ready to eat. Serve it as it is or dress it up with seasonal fruit, such as roasted rhubarb, or with something exotic such as mango.

SERVES 4

400ml double cream
90g golden caster sugar
juice and zest of 2
    unwaxed lemons

Lemon confit (optional)
thinly pared peel of 1
    unwaxed lemon, cut
    into fine matchsticks
150g golden caster sugar

1 For the lemon confit, if using, put the matchsticks of peel in a pan of boiling water, then drain and refresh them in cold water. Repeat this process 3 times to make a better-tasting confit. Put the sugar in a pan with 200ml of water and slowly bring it to the boil over a gentle heat. Add the boiled lemon peel and cook for 15–20 minutes. Strain off the liquid and leave the strips of lemon on greaseproof paper to cool.

2 Put the cream and sugar in a pan, place the pan over a gentle heat and slowly bring the cream to the boil. Simmer for 3 minutes, then take the pan off the heat, add the lemon juice and zest and whisk well.

3 Pour the mixture into 4 ramekins, then chill the possets in the fridge for 2–3 hours. Scatter with the lemon confit, if using, then serve with biscuits such as amaretti (see page 231).

PUDDINGS
& CAKES

♀ COOK'S TIP ♀
To help get as much juice as possible out of a lemon, first trim off the top and bottom, then cut the lemon in half and squeeze. You'll find it squeezes more easily.

CRÈME BRÛLÉE

This has always been one of my very favourite desserts. It's not one you can go skinny on, though – you have to use double cream. Ramekins are fine for this, but I sometimes like to use little eared dishes, which look so pretty. The ramekins or dishes should have a capacity of about 120ml. You can make the brûlées two or three days in advance, if you like, and add the topping at the last minute. Always serve them at room temperature for the best flavour.

SERVES 4

5 large egg yolks
50g golden caster
    sugar, plus extra
    for the caramel
400ml double cream
1 tsp vanilla bean paste

1 Preheat the oven to 160°C/Fan 140°C/Gas 3. Whisk the egg yolks with the 50g of sugar in a bowl until the mixture turns pale in colour.

2 Pour the cream into a pan. Add the vanilla bean paste, then bring to the boil. Pour the cream into the egg yolks and sugar mixture, whisking all the time.

3 Divide the mixture between 4 ramekins or dishes, leaving a little room at the top for the sugar topping. Put the ramekins or dishes in a baking tin and add just-boiled water to come two-thirds up the sides of the ramekins – or if using eared dishes, add water to a depth of about 1cm. Bake in the preheated oven for up to 1 hour but check after 45 minutes – they should still have a slight wobble.

4 Remove the brûlées and allow them to cool. Just before serving, sprinkle a thin layer of sugar over the surface of each one and melt the sugar with a cook's blowtorch or under a fierce grill, just enough for it to caramelise. On no account put the brûlées in the fridge once you've done this, or the tops will go soggy.

🍴 COOK'S TIP 🍴
If you like, you can add different fillings to the dishes, such as caramelised banana, raisins in rum, prunes in brandy, raspberries or prunes soaked in Armagnac, before pouring in the cream mixture.

CRÈME CARAMEL

An old-fashioned dessert but none the worse for that, this can be served with almond tuiles for a touch of trad glamour. It's easy to make but preparing the caramel can be challenging and needs a little practice. As this is made with half milk, half cream, it is lighter than crème brûlée.

SERVES 4

330g golden caster sugar
3 eggs
2 egg yolks
2 tsp vanilla bean paste
200ml double cream
200ml whole milk

1 Preheat the oven to 170°C/Fan 150°C/Gas 3½ and have 4 ramekin dishes ready.

2 First make the caramel. Put 250g of the sugar in a pan with 2 tablespoons of water and place the pan over a low heat. Once the sugar has dissolved, turn up the heat and cook until the mixture turns a light caramel colour, being very careful not to let it colour further. Have a bowl of cold water ready and put the base of the pan in this to stop the caramel cooking any more. Pour some caramel into each ramekin and swirl it around to coat the inside.

3 Whisk the eggs and yolks in a bowl with the remaining 80g of sugar and the vanilla bean paste until the mixture turns pale.

4 Pour the cream and milk into a pan and place over a gentle heat. Bring to simmering point, then remove from the heat and pour the cream and milk on to the egg mixture, whisking constantly. Divide the mixture between the ramekins. Take a piece of cling film and dip it quickly on top of each one to remove any air bubbles.

5 Place the ramekins in a roasting tin and add enough lukewarm water to come halfway up the sides of the dishes. Cook the crème caramels in the preheated oven for 25–30 minutes, then remove and leave to cool.

6 If you want to turn the crème caramels out, invert the dishes on to plates, tap the bases and they will slide out easily.

BREAD AND BUTTER PUDDING

Who doesn't love bread and butter pudding? I must say, though, that this is an indulgence and you have to use proper double cream – no place for a skinny version here! If you like, you can make this in advance, then cut it into quarters and reheat it in the oven to serve.

SERVES 4

60g sultanas
4 tbsp rum or fresh
    orange juice
60g butter, softened
8–10 slices of brioche
    or white bread,
    crusts removed
5 eggs
100g golden caster sugar
1 tsp vanilla extract
2 tsp ground cinnamon
200ml double cream
200ml whipping cream
demerara sugar,
    for dusting

1 First soak the sultanas in the rum or orange juice – the night before, if you can.

2 Butter a gratin dish or baking tin, roughly 26 x 19cm, with a little of the butter. Spread the brioche or bread generously with butter and cut each slice diagonally in half.

3 Whisk the eggs and sugar together in a bowl with the vanilla extract and the cinnamon. Put the double cream and whipping cream in a pan and heat gently until they reach simmering point. Pour them into the bowl with the eggs and sugar, whisking all the time.

4 Strain the sultanas and add the rum or orange juice soaking liquid to the egg and cream mixture. Layer the bread in the dish, overlapping the slices and sprinkling some sultanas over each layer. Pour the egg mixture over the bread and leave the dish in the fridge for 20 minutes for the bread to soak up the liquid – this is important, so don't be tempted to skip this step. Preheat the oven to 200°C/Fan 180°C/Gas 6.

5 Place the dish in a roasting tin and add just-boiled water to come about halfway up the sides. Cook the pudding in the preheated oven for 30–40 minutes, then remove and leave it to settle for 5 minutes. Sprinkle the top of the pudding with demerara sugar and put it under the grill or heat with a cook's blowtorch until lightly browned.

SWEET PASTRY

Many people are scared of making pastry but once you get the knack it is
so easy and very satisfying to do. The trick with pastry is to handle it as
little as possible and work quickly. For most tarts, you need to bake the
pastry case before adding the filling – a process known as 'blind baking'.
I generally use a flan ring on a silicone mat or a baking tray, as I find it makes
it easier to remove the tart, but you can also use a loose-bottomed flan tin.

**MAKES ENOUGH TO
LINE A 20–23CM TART
TIN OR RING**

110g cold unsalted butter,
    plus extra for greasing
200g plain flour, plus
    extra for dusting
1 egg
50g golden caster sugar

1 Cut the butter into small cubes, put them in a food
processor with the flour and pulse to the texture of
breadcrumbs. Add the egg, sugar and 2 tablespoons
of cold water, then process until the dough starts to
come together in a ball – don't overwork the dough.
Remove the dough from the bowl and shape it into a
cylinder. Wrap it in cling film and chill it in the fridge
for an hour.

2 If you want to make the pastry by hand, cut the
butter into tiny pieces and crumble them into the
flour with your fingertips until the mixture resembles
breadcrumbs. Add the rest of the ingredients and mix
to form a dough, then wrap the dough in cling film
and chill as above.

3 When ready to use, put the chilled pastry on a lightly
floured surface. Press it down slightly with the palm
of your hand, then roll it out into a large round about
2mm thick.

4 To blind bake the pastry case, butter the inside of a
20cm or 23cm ring or a loose-bottomed flan tin. If you
are using a ring, place it on a silicone baking mat or
a baking tray lined with baking paper. The edges of
a flan tin can be sharp so it's best to fold the pastry
in half, then again into a quarter, find the middle of
the tin, then unfold the pastry over the tin. Make sure
you get the pastry into the edges of the base. If you
are using a fluted tin, take a small ball of the excess
pastry, wrap it in cling film and use it to push the
pastry into the edges.

5   Once you have lined the tin, run the rolling pin lightly over the top to trim off any excess pastry. Then go round one more time, pressing the pastry gently up the sides so it comes about 5mm above the top of the tin or ring. Prick the base all over with a fork. Put the pastry in the fridge for 30 minutes. Preheat the oven to 200°C/Fan 180°C/Gas 6.

6   Take a large piece of greaseproof paper and screw it up so it is easier to get into the corners of the pastry. Place it over the pastry and fill it with baking beans, then bake in the preheated oven for 15 minutes. Remove the paper and beans, then put the pastry case back into the oven for about another 10 minutes or until pale golden brown. Remove and leave to cool.

♀ COOK'S TIP ♀

You can flavour your pastry if you like, adding lemon or orange zest, chocolate or spices to the dough.

PECAN AND CHOCOLATE TART

This pecan tart is made extra special and delicious by the layer of dark chocolate brushed over the base. Serve with some whipped cream for a real treat.

SERVES 8

70g dark chocolate
   (minimum 64%
   cocoa solids)
23cm pastry case,
   blind baked (see
   pages 220–21)
2 medium eggs
1 egg yolk
2 tsp vanilla extract
100g soft brown sugar
50g golden syrup
50g butter
175g pecan nuts, chopped
1 tbsp runny honey,
   to glaze

1 Preheat the oven to 200°C/Fan 180°C/Gas 6. Melt the chocolate in a bowl over a pan of gently simmering water. Don't let the water boil or allow the bottom of the bowl to touch the water or the chocolate may overheat. Brush the base of the pastry case with the melted chocolate.

2 Beat the eggs and egg yolk in a bowl, then stir in the vanilla extract, sugar and syrup until well combined. Melt the butter in a small pan and stir it into the eggs, then add the pecans and mix well.

3 Pour the mixture into the pastry case and bake in the preheated oven for 30–35 minutes. Remove the tart from the oven and allow to cool a little, then warm the honey and brush it over the tart.

BRAMLEY APPLE PIE

Bramleys are by far and away my favourite apples for cooking – you can't beat them for flavour. They do go mushy quickly, though, so keep a close eye on them when making the filling for this splendid pie.

SERVES 6–8

2kg Bramley apples
juice of 2 lemons
250g golden caster sugar,
    plus extra for dusting
2 tsp ground cinnamon
50g unsalted butter

Pastry
350g plain flour, plus
    extra for dusting
150g cold unsalted butter,
    cut into small cubes
2 tbsp golden caster sugar
1 egg, beaten with 1 tbsp
    whole milk, to glaze

1 First make the pastry. Pulse the flour and butter in a food processor until the mixture resembles breadcrumbs or put the flour in a bowl and rub in the cubes of butter with your fingertips. Add the sugar and 160ml of cold water and mix or process the mixture into a dough. Wrap the dough in cling film and leave it to chill in the fridge while you prepare the filling.

2 Peel and core the apples and cut them into thick slices, then put them in a pan with the lemon juice and sugar. Bring to a simmer over a low heat and cook for 2 minutes only – don't cook them too long. Tip them into a sieve over a bowl to drain the juice, then set aside to cool. Fold in the cinnamon.

3 Preheat the oven to 200°C/Fan 180°C/Gas 6. Grease a 22cm shallow pie dish with a little of the butter. Cut the pastry in two – one piece slightly bigger than the other – and put them on a lightly floured work surface. Roll out the smaller piece to fit the pie dish, allowing enough to overhang the sides. Roll out the other half, ready to put over the top of the pie.

4 Fill the lined pie dish with layers of cooled apple slices, piling them up high. Be patient about doing this and it might seem ridiculously high but, trust me, this works. Dot with the remaining butter. Brush the pastry edges with some of the beaten egg mixture, place the pastry lid on top and press all round to make sure the edges are well sealed.

5 Using a sharp knife, trim off the excess pastry. Brush the pie with the rest of the beaten egg and cut a steam hole, about 5mm in diameter, in the middle. Dust with caster sugar, then bake the pie in the preheated oven for 40–45 minutes, until golden.

CHRISTMAS TART

Some members of my family aren't keen on Christmas pudding and this is a great alternative. It's based on a delicious tart I ate in Scotland many years ago and it's easy to make. If you prefer, you can make little individual tarts, which look very pretty. You'll need one and a half times the sweet pastry recipe so you have enough for the lattice – use one egg and an extra yolk.

SERVES 8

350g mixed dried fruit
50g candied peel
40ml rum
2 eggs
180g soft brown sugar
1 tbsp red wine vinegar
150g butter
2 tsp ground cinnamon
1 tsp grated nutmeg
100g chopped walnuts
23cm pastry case, blind baked (see pages 220–21), plus extra pastry for the lattice (see introduction above)
plain flour, for dusting
beaten egg, to glaze

1 Put the dried fruit and candied peel in a bowl, stir in the rum and leave to soak for 30 minutes.

2 Preheat the oven to 180°C/Fan 160°C/Gas 4. Whisk the eggs and sugar with the vinegar. Melt the butter in a small pan, then whisk it into the egg mixture. Add the dried fruit and the rum, then the spices and walnuts, and mix well. Tip the mixture into a food processor and pulse, being careful not to process it too much – you want a roughly chopped mixture with some texture, not a purée. Scoop the mixture into the pastry case.

3 Take the extra pastry and, on a lightly floured worktop, roll it out into an oblong shape and use a lattice cutter to create your lattice. Carefully place this over the tart, trim and press the edges together to secure them. If you don't have a lattice cutter, cut the pastry into 1cm strips. Place some strips across the tart, leaving 2cm between each one and pressing them gently on to the pastry rim to secure. Then add another series of strips across them to make a lattice pattern. Brush the pastry with beaten egg.

4 Bake the tart in the preheated oven for 45 minutes. Remove and feel the centre – if there is no bounce, it's done. Serve hot or cold.

BAKEWELL TART

A classic tart seen in so many cafés, this is so much better when you bake it yourself. I think it's a great standby pudding, as it is made with store-cupboard ingredients that most of us have to hand. It's simple but utterly delicious.

SERVES 6

20cm pastry case,
    blind baked (see
    pages 220–21)

Filling
3 eggs
100g golden caster sugar
150g butter, melted
    and cooled
120g ground almonds
1 tsp almond extract
finely grated zest of
    ½ lemon
2 heaped tbsp unseeded
    raspberry jam
icing sugar, for dusting

1 Preheat the oven to 150°C/Fan 130°C/Gas 2. First make the almond filling. Beat the eggs and sugar together in a bowl until they turn slightly paler in colour. Stir in the melted butter, ground almonds, almond extract and lemon zest.

2 Spread the raspberry jam over the base of the pastry case and top with the almond filling. Cook the tart in the preheated oven for 30–40 minutes until the filling is lightly coloured and a skewer inserted in the centre comes out clean. Remove and allow to cool completely. Dust with icing sugar before serving.

LEMON AND SOFT FRUIT TART

This tart looks so pretty and makes a delightful summer dessert. If you prefer, you could make six small tarts in individual tartlet cases or rings.

SERVES 6

23cm pastry case, baked
   blind (see pages 220–21)
300g raspberries
150g blueberries
icing sugar, for dusting
mint leaves, to decorate
   (optional)

Lemon pâtissière
2 eggs
2 tbsp lemon juice
60g golden caster sugar
25g unsalted butter

1 First make the lemon pâtissière. Beat the eggs in a large bowl. Put the lemon juice in a pan with the sugar, place it over a low heat to just dissolve the sugar, then bring it to the boil. Take the pan off the heat and beat in the butter, then whisk this mixture into the bowl with the eggs.

2 Pour everything back into the pan, place the pan over a low heat and very slowly bring everything to a simmer, whisking all the time. Pour the mixture into a bowl and cover with cling film, making sure the film touches the mixture so condensation cannot form. Set aside to cool.

3 Fill the pastry case with the lemon pâtissière and arrange the soft fruit on top. Scatter with mint leaves, if using, and dust with icing sugar.

TREACLE AND GINGER TART

Treacle tart is a classic of British cooking and one of our best desserts. I love the touch of ginger in this recipe. Spoil yourself and serve the tart with clotted cream or vanilla ice cream.

SERVES 6

2 balls of stem ginger in syrup, drained
400g golden syrup
juice and zest of 1 lemon
150g breadcrumbs
1 tsp ground ginger
20cm pastry case, blind baked (see pages 220–21)

1 Preheat the oven to 190°C/Fan 170°C/Gas 5. Finely chop or grate the stem ginger.

2 Mix the chopped ginger with the golden syrup, lemon juice and zest, breadcrumbs and ground ginger in a bowl, then pour the mixture into the pastry case.

3 Bake the tart in the preheated oven for 25–30 minutes or until pale golden brown. Remove and allow to cool before serving.

PARADISE TART

This is my mother's recipe for a pudding I love – it's very old-fashioned but absolutely delicious. I find it makes a nice alternative to traditional mince pies at Christmas.

SERVES 6

100g butter, at room temperature
100g golden caster sugar
1 egg
75g ground almonds
100g sultanas
75g glacé cherries (natural colour), chopped
75g walnut halves, chopped
40g rice flour
2 tsp vanilla extract
20cm pastry case, blind baked (see pages 220–21)

1 Preheat the oven to 200°C/Fan 180°C/Gas 6. Mix the butter, sugar and egg together in a bowl with an electric hand mixer. Add the ground almonds, sultanas and the chopped cherries and walnuts, then stir in the rice flour and vanilla extract. Pour the mixture into the pastry case.

2 Bake in the preheated oven for 35 minutes until set. Remove and serve with cream.

AMARETTI BISCUITS

These little biscuits are crispy on the outside but have a deliciously chewy centre. They're expensive to buy but simple to make yourself at home, and if you package them up nicely, they make lovely presents. Do be sure to leave the raw mixture to firm up. This allows time for the moisture to be absorbed and makes the mixture easier to shape.

MAKES ABOUT 36 BISCUITS

125g finely chopped
  hazelnuts
125g finely chopped
  almonds
160g golden caster sugar
1 level tsp amaretto or
  ½ tsp almond extract
3 medium egg whites

1 Put the hazelnuts, almonds, half the sugar and the amaretto or almond extract in a large bowl. Whisk the egg whites to soft peaks in a separate, spotlessly clean bowl, then add them to the nut mixture and stir until combined.

2 Cover the bowl and leave it in the fridge for 12 hours or until the mixture is firm. Line a couple of baking sheets with baking paper.

3 Preheat the oven to 200°C/Fan 180°C/Gas 6. Spread the remaining sugar in a shallow dish. Roll the mixture into small balls, each slightly smaller than a walnut, and roll them in the dish of sugar until evenly coated.

4 Place the coated balls on the lined baking sheets, spacing them about 3cm apart. Bake them in the preheated oven for 12–15 minutes until golden brown. Leave the biscuits to cool for a couple of minutes on the baking sheets, then transfer them to a wire rack to cool completely.

CARROT CAKE WITH ORANGE BUTTERCREAM AND WALNUTS

I always enjoy carrot cake but this one is made extra special by the addition of dates, which give it a slightly Middle Eastern flavour. It is worth adding the carrot confit if you have time, as it looks pretty and tastes great.

SERVES 8

200g plain flour
2 slightly heaped tsp
    bicarbonate of soda
100g walnuts, roughly
    chopped, plus some
    extra walnut halves
    to decorate
250g runny honey
100g carrots, peeled
    and finely grated
180g pitted dates, chopped
2 tsp ground cinnamon
1 tsp grated nutmeg
100g butter, plus extra
    for greasing

Buttercream icing
250g unsalted butter,
    at room temperature
500g icing sugar, sifted
finely grated zest of
    1 well-washed orange
100ml double cream

Carrot confit (optional)
150g golden caster sugar
1 large carrot, peeled
    and cut into fine
    matchsticks

1 First put the flour, bicarbonate of soda and the roughly chopped walnuts in a large bowl and set it aside. Preheat the oven to 180°C/Fan 160°C/Gas 4.

2 Put the honey, carrots, dates, cinnamon, nutmeg and butter in a pan and add 200ml of water. Place the pan over a gentle heat and let everything melt together, then simmer for 5–7 minutes. Tip the mixture into a bowl and leave to cool until lukewarm. Then add the flour, bicarb and walnuts to the carrot mixture and stir well.

3 Grease a 22cm loose-bottomed cake tin and line the base and sides with baking paper. Pour in the cake mixture, then bake the cake in the preheated oven for 45 minutes or until firm to the touch. Remove the cake from the oven and allow it to cool for 5 minutes, then transfer it to a wire rack to cool completely.

4 To make the buttercream, put the butter in a bowl with the icing sugar and orange zest. Using an electric hand mixer, beat until soft. Whisk the cream to soft peaks and fold it into the butter and sugar mixture.

5 To make the confit carrot, if using, put the sugar in a pan with 200ml of water and slowly bring to the boil over a gentle heat. Add the carrot and cook for 15–20 minutes. Strain off the liquid and leave the strips of carrot on a piece of greaseproof paper to cool.

6 To assemble the cake, cut it in half horizontally. Spread some of the buttercream on the bottom layer, cover with the other half of the cake and spread the rest of the icing on top. Then decorate with the walnut halves and the carrot confit, if using.

BEETROOT BROWNIES

You can, of course, make these with ordinary flour and baking powder but I'm often asked for gluten-free recipes and this works well. Beetroot goes beautifully with chocolate and creates a lovely moist cake. By the way, if you want to cook your own beetroot, make sure it is really soft, so it makes a nice purée.

MAKES 12 SQUARES

300g cooked beetroot
    (vacuum-packed is fine)
butter, for greasing
150g gluten-free white
    bread flour
45g cocoa powder
1 tsp ground cinnamon
½ tsp bicarbonate of soda
1 tsp gluten-free
    baking powder
¼ tsp fine sea salt
250ml maple syrup
100ml whole milk
1 tsp vanilla bean paste

1 Put the beetroot in a blender and blitz it to form a purée, then pass the purée through a fine sieve into a bowl. Preheat the oven to 180°C/Fan 160°C/Gas 4. Grease a 28 x 18cm baking tin with butter and line it with non-stick baking paper.

2 Put the flour, cocoa powder, cinnamon, bicarbonate of soda, baking powder and salt in a bowl and mix well with a whisk – whisking will prevent any lumps forming in the flour. Add the beetroot purée, maple syrup, milk and vanilla bean paste and mix well with a spatula until combined.

3 Pour the mixture into the lined baking tin and bake in the preheated oven for 25–30 minutes. Place the tin on a wire rack and leave the brownies to cool, then cut them into 12 squares.

LIME AND GINGER DRIZZLE CAKE

I always think of lemon drizzle as such a typically British cake, but in fact this method of adding flavoursome syrup is popular all over Europe and the Middle East. And if you like, you can ring the changes with the flavour, adding dried lavender or star anise instead of ginger to the syrup. I love this cake as a dessert as well as for tea – it's delicious served with pistachio ice cream.

SERVES

200g butter, softened,
   plus extra for greasing
200g golden caster sugar
1 lemon
4 limes
3 eggs, lightly beaten
200g self-raising flour
1 tsp baking powder
1 tsp ground ginger
4 balls of stem ginger in
   syrup, drained,
    2 tbsp syrup reserved
3 tbsp whole milk
100g granulated sugar

1 Preheat the oven to 180°C/Fan 160°C/Gas 4. Grease a 900g loaf tin and line it with baking paper.

2 Using an electric hand mixer, cream the butter and caster sugar together until pale, light and fluffy. Finely grate the zest of the lemon and 2 of the limes and add it to the mixture.

3 Add the eggs, one at a time, adding a spoonful of flour each time and mixing well in between each addition. In a separate bowl, whisk the rest of the flour with the baking powder and ground ginger, then stir this into the cake batter.

4 Chop 3 of the balls of stem ginger and fold them into the cake batter with a spatula. Add the milk and the juice from 2 of the limes and mix until smooth. Spoon the mixture into the prepared tin and bake for about 55 minutes. To check, insert a skewer into the middle of the cake and it should come out clean. If not, put the cake back in the oven for another 5 minutes or so. Cool the cake in the tin for 10 minutes while you make the syrup.

5 Put the juice of the remaining 2 limes and the lemon in a small pan with the ginger syrup and granulated sugar. Place over a gentle heat to dissolve the sugar and combine the ingredients. Make holes all over the top of the cake with a skewer, then spoon the sugary syrup over the cake. Leave it in the tin to cool completely. Chop the remaining ball of stem ginger and sprinkle it over the cake before serving.

CHOCOLATE FONDANTS

I know people are a bit scared about making these, fearing they won't achieve the melting chocolatey middles, but once you get the timing right, fondants are really easy to do. They're well worth practising as they are a great store-cupboard standby and everyone enjoys them. Dariole moulds are the ideal containers but you can also use ramekins.

SERVES 4

spray oil or 25g
   butter, melted
50g cocoa powder
120g dark chocolate
   (minimum 64% cocoa
   solids), broken up
70g butter, diced
75g golden caster sugar
2 eggs
15g plain flour

1 Spray the insides of 4 dariole moulds or ramekins with oil or brush them with melted butter, then dust them lightly with some of the cocoa powder. This will prevent the fondant from sticking after baking. Preheat the oven to 200°C/Fan 180°C/Gas 6.

2 You need a pan and a heatproof bowl that fits neatly over it. Bring some water to simmering point in the pan, then put the bowl on top, making sure the bottom of the bowl doesn't touch the water. Add the chocolate and diced butter and allow them to melt gently. Don't let the water boil, as this could burn the chocolate. Ideally, test the chocolate with a sugar thermometer – it should reach 55°C. Remove the pan and bowl from the heat and allow the melted chocolate and butter to cool slightly.

3 Using an electric hand mixer, mix the sugar and eggs in a bowl until they have doubled in size and are pale in colour. Add the flour and whisk again until there are no lumps. Add the melted chocolate and butter and mix until well combined. Fill the moulds or ramekins about three-quarters full.

4 Place the moulds or ramekins on a baking tray and bake in the preheated oven for 9 minutes. Remove them and leave to rest for 2 minutes, then turn them out on to plates. Dust with the rest of the cocoa powder and serve at once – with a dollop of vanilla ice cream, if you fancy.

PEAR TARTE TATIN

A French favourite, this is an upside-down tart – the fruit is caramelised and then covered with a blanket of puff pastry before baking. When the tart is cooked, it is inverted on to a plate in all its sticky glory. You can use any pears, but I think Williams are best. A great show-off dish.

SERVES 4–6

4 pears
juice of 1 lemon
125g golden caster sugar
4 tbsp Poire Williams
    liqueur (or brandy
    or rum), warmed
75g butter, diced
375g packet of puff pastry
plain flour, for dusting

1 Peel and core the pears, then cut them into slices. Place the slices in a bowl of cold water and add the lemon juice and squeezed lemon halves. This stops the pears going brown.

2 Place a 24cm ovenproof frying pan over a medium-to-low heat. Add the sugar and let it melt – avoid stirring at this stage as it can make the sugar crystallise. When a pale caramel, about the colour of golden syrup, has formed, add the warmed Poire Williams (or brandy or rum) and swirl the pan around. Add the butter, swirling the pan all the time until the mixture has amalgamated – be careful not to burn yourself.

3 Drain the pear slices and pat them dry, then arrange over the caramel, fanning them out as neatly as you can. Preheat the oven to 220°C/Fan 200°C/Gas 7.

4 Roll out the puff pastry on a lightly floured surface to make a circle 2cm wider than the frying pan and about 4mm thick. Place the pastry over the pears and tuck it in around the sides.

5 Put the frying pan in the preheated oven and bake the tart for 25–35 minutes. Have a look at it and if the pastry has risen nicely and is golden brown, remove the tart from the oven. If not, leave it in the oven for another 5–10 minutes.

6 Leave the tart to stand for 10 minutes. Take a plate that's slightly larger than the pan and place it over the pan, then carefully turn the pan over to invert the tart on to the plate. Wear oven gloves so you don't burn yourself!

PUDDINGS
& CAKES

CHOCOLATE AND CARDAMOM MOUSSE

I think that chocolate and cardamom are divine together and this is an excellent, flavoursome mousse. It's ideal for a party as you can make it in advance, and if you make more than you need, it freezes like a dream. I've given weights for the egg yolks and whites, as it is important to have the right quantities for this recipe to work.

SERVES 6

12 cardamom pods
200g dark chocolate
   (minimum 64%
   cocoa solids)
300g whipping cream
90g egg whites and
   60g egg yolks
   (3 medium eggs)
75g golden caster sugar

Topping (optional)
whipped cream
chocolate shavings

1 Remove the seeds from the cardamom pods and discard the husks. Place the seeds in a dry pan and toast them over a medium heat for 30 seconds, then grind them to a fine powder with a pestle and mortar or in a spice grinder.

2 Now melt the chocolate. You need a pan and a heatproof bowl that fits neatly over it. Bring some water to simmering point in the pan, then put the bowl on top, making sure the bottom of the bowl doesn't touch the water. Add the chocolate and allow it to melt gently. Don't let the water boil, as this could burn the chocolate.

3 When the chocolate has melted, remove the bowl from the pan. Add the ground cardamom seeds and give the chocolate a good stir, then set it aside to cool slightly.

4 Put the cream in a separate bowl and whisk to thicken slightly, then set it aside. Whisk the egg whites to stiff peaks, then set them aside too.

5 Place the sugar and egg yolks in a large bowl and whisk until the sugar has dissolved and the egg yolks have thickened and gone almost white in colour. Add the melted chocolate, then the cream. Using a large metal spoon, fold in the whisked egg whites, being careful not to knock the air out.

6 Spoon the lovely light mousse into 6 ramekins or one large dish and leave in the fridge to chill for at least 2 hours until set. Serve topped with whipped cream and chocolate shavings, if you like.

STRAWBERRY AND LAVENDER CRUMBLE TRIFLE

Trifle is such a quintessentially British dish and this exquisite version is worthy of a special occasion. Yes, there is quite a bit of work, but you can make the jelly and custard in advance and have the crumble ready to add just before you serve the trifles. They're best in glass containers so you can see the lovely layers.

SERVES 4

Strawberry and lavender jelly
500g strawberries, hulled
100g golden caster sugar
5g edible dried lavender
6g gelatine leaves

Crumble
40g plain flour
20g golden caster sugar
30g demerara sugar
35g rolled oats
40g butter, diced

Macerated strawberries
12 large or 16 medium
    strawberries, hulled
75g golden caster sugar
1 tbsp vanilla bean paste
juice of ½ lime

Custard
500ml whole milk
1 tbsp vanilla bean paste
5 egg yolks
100g golden caster sugar
10g plain flour
40g custard powder

Chantilly cream
250ml double cream
1 tbsp vanilla bean paste
30g icing sugar

1 First make the jelly. Put the strawberries, sugar and lavender in a pan and cover the pan with cling film. Place over a medium heat and bring to a simmer – do not allow to boil – then simmer for 10–15 minutes. Remove the pan from the heat and set the mixture aside to infuse for 15 minutes, then pass it through a sieve. You will be left with a nice clear lavender-flavoured strawberry juice. Measure out 250ml of the juice.

2 Soak the gelatine leaves in a bowl of cold water for 5 minutes. Pour the 250ml of juice back into the pan, heat it through gently, then remove the pan from the heat. Squeeze the excess water from the gelatine leaves, add them to the strawberry liquid, then stir to dissolve. Pass the liquid through a fine sieve, then into 4 glasses and put them in the fridge to chill until set.

3 For the crumble, preheat the oven to 150°C/Fan 130°C/ Gas 2. Put the flour, sugars, oats and butter in a food processor and blend until the mixture resembles breadcrumbs. Line a baking tray with baking paper and scatter the crumble over it. Bake for 40 minutes, turning the mix every 10 minutes or so. Keep a close eye on it so it doesn't burn. Remove from the oven and leave to cool. Crumble the mixture with your fingers and set it aside until ready to serve.

4 For the macerated strawberries, cut the strawberries in halves or quarters, depending on their size, and put them in a bowl. Put the sugar, vanilla paste and lime juice in a pan with a tablespoon of water and warm gently to dissolve the sugar. Pour the mixture over the strawberries and leave to infuse.

5 For the custard, pour the milk into a pan, add the vanilla paste and bring to a low simmer. Meanwhile, whisk the egg yolks, sugar, flour and custard powder together in a heatproof bowl. Pour the hot milk, a little at a time, into the egg mixture, whisking constantly. Return the custard to the pan and cook over a low heat until it thickens, stirring constantly. Remove from the heat, put a layer of cling film over the surface to prevent a skin forming and leave to cool.

6 For the chantilly cream, whisk the cream, vanilla bean paste and icing sugar in a bowl until soft peaks form.

7 To assemble the trifles, top the jelly with a layer of drained macerated strawberries, then spoon on some custard, then some cream and sprinkle with the crumble mixture. Serve immediately.

BREAD

The chapter begins with the basics, then progresses, skill by skill, recipe by recipe, up to showpiece breads that really wow.

THERE'S NOTHING AS MOUTHWATERING AS THE SMELL OF a loaf of bread baking in the oven. I think that bread is the most magical, amazing thing to cook. I find it fascinating that you can take the simplest ingredients – flour, yeast, water and salt – and make something so delicious. I bake bread regularly and, like many things, once you get the knack it's easy and so rewarding. With bread, practice really does make perfect.

One of the many huge advantages in making your own bread is that you know exactly what goes into it. Look at the long list of ingredients in a commercial loaf and you'll see a host of preservatives and emulsifiers that extend shelf life but have no nutritional value and certainly do nothing for the taste and quality of the bread. At home, you have no need of these extras and you can make bread the way it should be made, with just flour, yeast, water and salt.

FLOUR
Using good-quality flour is very important. I do feel you get what you pay for when it comes to flour and I advise finding a good supplier and sticking with it.

I like to use traditional stoneground flour (as opposed to flour milled between steel rollers), as it still contains some wheatgerm and bran, so is higher in fibre and nutrients. Also stoneground white flour is not bleached, unlike ordinary white flour. I generally add some white flour to wholemeal or rye to make my bread lighter.

You will see flour labelled 'strong flour' or 'strong bread flour'. This means that it contains more gluten than ordinary flour, which gives it elasticity and helps the dough to rise better.

Organic flour is made from grain grown by organic methods, with no use of artificial fertilisers and pesticides.

RAISING AGENTS
There are three different raising agents for bread: yeast (dried or fresh); bicarbonate of soda for instant bread like soda bread, which requires no kneading; and natural fermentation, as in sourdough bread.

In the following recipes I have given quantities for fast-action dried yeast, which is very convenient, but I do like to use fresh yeast when I can. You can buy it from supermarkets – ask at the bread counter – and it keeps for about three weeks. The following gives you an idea of equivalent amounts.

Fast-action yeast	Fresh yeast
1g	3g
2g	6g
3g	10g
4g	12g
5g	17g
7g	23g
10g	34g

KNEADING
Good kneading technique is the key to great breadmaking and it is kneading that gets the gluten in the flour working

with the yeast. As you tear and knead the dough, you create strands that make it stretchy and elastic and allow the dough to rise as the yeast ferments. You should knead your dough for 10–15 minutes, but generally the longer you knead, the better the bread.

RISING

Once the dough has been kneaded you have to leave it to rise or prove. First put the bowl of dough in a plastic bag or cover it with cling film – this is important as it creates condensation, and if the dough is not covered it will form a crust on top. Leave the bowl in the warm kitchen, out of the way of draughts but not near anything hot, such as an Aga. Many people think you should put dough to prove somewhere like an airing cupboard, but that is often too warm and makes the dough rise too quickly.

The time dough takes to rise will vary, depending first on the temperature of the room and second, the ingredients. If the room is cool, the dough will take longer to rise. Wholemeal flour takes longer to rise than white and if you've added heavy flavourings, the rising time will be longer.

It's important that the dough should not over-prove. It should still look smooth, and if you see strands beginning to form that's a sign of over-proving and the bread won't rise as well.

After the first rise or prove, the dough must be knocked back to push some of the air out and stabilise it before the second rise, during which the volume and flavour improves

IDEAS FOR FLAVOURING BREAD ROLLS

Once you have made some of the simple breads in this chapter and have an idea of how dough should be, you can have fun experimenting with adding different ingredients. Use the French sticks recipe on page 257, but make it into rolls weighing about 50 grams each. Cook them for 12 minutes at 240°C/Fan 220°C/Gas 9.

Flavours to add before the first rise

- **Bacon and onion:** Cut 3 rashers of bacon and half a Spanish onion into small dice. Brown the bacon in a little oil in a pan, then set it aside while you cook the onion. Put the bacon and onion in a bowl and leave them to cool, then add them to the dough before the first rise.
- **Black olives:** Finely chop 150g pitted black olives and add them to the dough before the first rise. This does make rolls with a strong olive flavour, so reduce the quantity if you prefer.
- **Black pudding:** Crumble 200g black pudding into the dough before the first rise.
- **Saffron:** Steep a good pinch of saffron in a tablespoon of just-boiled water for half an hour. Add it to the water for the bread.

Coatings for rolls to add before the second rise

Choose from poppy seeds, sesame seeds, sunflower seeds, cumin seeds, nigella seeds, oats, polenta, grated cheese or chopped herbs.

Have a bowl of water ready and the flavouring of your choice in a separate dish. Take a roll, dip it into the water, then into the coating.

☆ COOK'S TIP ☆

When you put your bread in the oven, spray a little water into the oven to create steam or simply put a bowl of water in the bottom of the oven. This will give your bread a better crust.

WHITE LOAF

This makes a regular, all-purpose white country loaf, good
for sandwiches and toast. It's my kitchen standby.

MAKES 2 LOAVES

900g strong white
   bread flour, plus
   extra for dusting
50g cold butter, diced
12g fast-action dried yeast
600ml water, room
   temperature
15g fine sea salt
vegetable oil, for greasing

1 Put the flour in a large bowl and rub in the cold
butter until the texture resembles breadcrumbs.
Add the yeast and mix well, then add the water
and mix to a dough.

2 Tip the dough on to a lightly floured work surface.
Clean your hands and dust them with flour. Knead
the dough by placing the 3 middle fingers of your left
hand on the bottom part of the dough, then, using the
palm of the other hand, push the dough away from
you. Roll the dough back towards you and give it a
half turn. Repeat the process for 10 minutes, kneading
in the salt halfway through and remembering to give
the dough a half turn each time.

3 Dust a bowl with flour, then roll the dough into a ball
and put it in the bowl. Cover the bowl with cling film
and leave the dough at room temperature to double
in size.

4 Oil 2 x 900g loaf tins. Knock the dough back by
kneading it again 3 times, then cut it into 2 pieces
and put them in the prepared tins. Leave them to
rise again for about 45 minutes. Preheat the oven
to 240°C/Fan 220°C/Gas 9.

5 Bake the bread in the preheated oven for 20 minutes,
then turn the temperature down to 170°C/Fan 150°C/
Gas 3½ and cook for a further 30 minutes. Remove a
loaf and tap the base – if it sounds hollow, it's done.
Cool the loaves on a wire rack.

SODA BREAD WITH RICOTTA

Soda bread is the quickest, easiest bread to make. One day, I just decided to add ricotta to the dough and I was delighted with the results, so I've done it ever since.

MAKES 2 LOAVES

550g plain flour, plus extra for dusting
1 tsp fine sea salt
1½ tsp bicarbonate of soda
450ml buttermilk
150g ricotta
1 tbsp sunflower oil

1 Preheat the oven to 220°C/Fan 200°C/Gas 7. Mix the flour, salt and bicarbonate of soda in a bowl, then add the buttermilk, ricotta and oil. Mix lightly and quickly to make a soft but not sticky dough.

2 Turn the dough out on to a well-floured work surface, then divide it into 2 pieces. Shape them into round loaves and place them on well-floured baking trays. Using a floured wooden spoon, mark a deep cross in each loaf.

3 Bake the bread in the preheated oven for 30 minutes. Remove and insert a metal skewer into the centre of one loaf. If it comes out clean, the bread is ready. Cool the loaves on a wire rack.

PIZZA

The best pizza I ever ate was in a large indoor market in Adelaide, Australia. Every bit was freshly made and it was simply delicious. Home-made pizzas are the best and the great thing is that you know exactly what goes into them! Always a treat, and children love to help and add their own toppings.

MAKES 3 PIZZAS

500g strong white flour,
    plus extra for dusting
7g fast-action dried yeast
1 tsp fine sea salt
300ml water, room
    temperature
sunflower oil, for greasing

Tomato sauce
1 tbsp olive oil
1 large onion, peeled
    and finely chopped
2 garlic cloves, peeled
    and finely chopped
800g beef tomatoes,
    peeled and chopped
2 tsp golden caster sugar
2 thyme sprigs
1 bay leaf
4 drops of Tabasco sauce
1 tbsp tomato pureé
fine sea salt and
    black pepper

Topping suggestion
1 tbsp olive oil
2 x 80g packs of
    Parma ham
2 x 125g balls of
    mozzarella
fresh basil leaves

1 To make the tomato sauce, heat the oil in a pan and gently soften the onion and garlic over a low heat. Add the tomatoes, sugar, thyme, bay leaf and Tabasco, then cover the pan and cook for about 10 minutes until the tomatoes have released their juices. Remove the lid and continue to cook for another 10 minutes until the mixture has thickened and the liquid has evaporated. Add the tomato purée and cook for couple of minutes longer. Remove the thyme sprigs, then tip the sauce into a food processor and blitz to a purée. Season with salt and pepper and set aside until required. You will have more sauce than you need, but it's always useful and freezes well.

2 For the pizza dough, put the flour in a large bowl. Add the yeast, salt and water and mix with your hands to make a slightly wet and workable dough. Tip the dough on to a lightly floured work surface. Clean your hands and lightly dust them with flour.

3 Knead the dough by placing the 3 middle fingers of your left hand on the bottom part of the dough, then, using the palm of the other hand, push the dough away from you. Roll the dough back towards you and give it a half turn. Repeat the process for 10 minutes, remembering to give the dough a half turn each time.

4 Place the dough in a clean, lightly floured bowl, cover it with cling film and leave it to rise until doubled in size. Knock back the dough by tipping it back on to a floured surface and kneading it again 3 times.

5 Divide the dough into 3 pieces and, using a rolling pin, roll them out as thinly as you can, trying to keep a nice round shape. Preheat the oven to 240°C/220°C Fan/Gas 9.

6 Spread 3–4 tablespoons of tomato sauce over each pizza base, then add whatever topping you desire. One of my favourites is Parma ham and mozzarella. Bake in the preheated oven for 10–15 minutes, depending on the thickness of your topping, then remove and sprinkle with fresh basil.

HERB FLATBREADS

These flatbreads are a really handy thing to have in your repertoire, as everyone enjoys them and they look so attractive. You do need to allow time for them to rise, but they are quick to cook, so if you get yourself organised, you can have delicious warm bread on the table for lunch.

MAKES 4 FLATBREADS

250g strong white flour, plus extra for dusting
7g fast-action dried yeast
2 tbsp chopped coriander or herb of your choice
3 tbsp olive oil
150ml water, room temperature
1 tsp fine sea salt

1 Put the flour and dried yeast in a bowl and mix them together with your hands. Add the chopped herbs and mix again. Add the oil and water to the flour, then using one hand, start to bring the dough together. Add the salt and work that into the dough. Don't worry if the dough is very sticky and wet; the kneading process will bring it together.

2 Tip the dough on to a lightly floured work surface. Clean your hands and dust them with flour. Knead the dough by placing the 3 middle fingers of your left hand on the bottom part of the dough, then, using the palm of the other hand, push the dough away from you. Roll the dough back towards you and give it a half turn. Repeat the process for 5 minutes, remembering to give the dough a half turn each time.

3 Sprinkle some flour into a clean bowl, roll the dough into a ball and put it in the bowl. Cover with cling film and leave it at room temperature to double in size.

4 Once the dough has doubled in size, tip it on to a lightly floured surface and knock it back by kneading it again 3 times. Roll the dough back into a ball, then cut it into 4 even portions. Roll these into balls.

5 Using a lightly floured rolling pin, roll out each piece of dough into a rough circle about 3mm thick. Leave them to prove again for 5 minutes.

6 Place a frying pan over a medium-high heat. Once it is hot, put a piece of dough straight into the dry pan. It should start to bubble on top. Leave it for 2 minutes, then turn it over and cook for another 2 minutes. Place the bread on a wire rack while you cook the rest in the same way. The bread should be nicely browned and crisp on the outside but soft and fluffy inside.

POTATO BREAD

These are like potato farls, a delicious type of bread made with mashed potato as well as flour. They're a lovely thing to serve for Sunday brunch, and with melted butter and poached eggs they're my idea of heaven! You can also make mini versions and top them with smoked salmon to serve as canapés.

MAKES 4 SQUARES

650g floury potatoes,
    such as Desirée, peeled
    and quartered
30g butter, melted
180g plain flour, plus
    extra for dusting
fine sea salt

1 Rinse the potatoes under cold running water for a couple of minutes to wash off any excess starch. Put them in a pan of cold water, add salt and place over a high heat. Bring to the boil, then turn the heat down to medium and cook the potatoes for about 15 minutes or until soft.

2 Drain the potatoes and leave them for 2 minutes to dry out a little. Mash until really smooth, then weigh out 480g of mashed potato. Put this in a bowl, add the melted butter and ½ teaspoon of salt, then work in the flour to make a pliable dough.

3 Turn the dough out on to a lightly floured surface and roll the dough out into a square measuring about 23cm and 5mm thick. Cut into 4 squares or smaller pieces, if you prefer.

4 Place a griddle pan or frying pan over a medium-high heat. When it's hot, put the pieces of dough straight on to the pan and cook them until lightly browned on both sides. They should take about 3 minutes each side. Good hot, cold or warm.

♀ COOK'S TIP ♀

To test if the pan is hot enough, dust it with a little flour. If it turns golden it is ready.

FRENCH STICKS

To make good bread you need good-quality flour – I never stint on flour. This is particularly true for French sticks, or baguettes, and the best flour to use is a French type known as T65. Failing this, choose a good-quality strong white bread flour from a local mill if possible.

MAKES 3 FRENCH STICKS

600g strong white flour (preferably French T65), plus extra for dusting
10g fast-action dried yeast
360ml water, room temperature
15g sea salt

1 Put the flour and dried yeast into a bowl and mix them together with your hands. Add the water and then, using one hand, start to bring the dough together. At this point add the salt and work it into the dough. Don't worry if the dough is very sticky and wet, the kneading process will bring it together.

2 Tip the dough on to a lightly floured work surface. Clean your hands and dust them with flour. Knead the dough by placing the 3 middle fingers of your left hand on the bottom part of the dough, then, using the palm of the other hand, push the dough away from you. Roll the dough back towards you and give it a half turn. Repeat the process for 10 minutes, remembering to give the dough a half turn each time.

3 Dust a bowl with flour, then roll the dough into a ball and put it in the bowl. Cover with cling film and leave the dough at room temperature to double in size.

4 Once the dough has doubled in size, tip it on to a lightly floured surface and knock it back by kneading it briefly. Roll the dough into a ball and cut it into 3 even portions. Roll these into long baguettes and slash each one across 3 times.

5 Place the loaves on a floured baking tray and leave them to rise again. Be sure to leave enough space between each stick, as they will double in size. Preheat the oven to 240°C/Fan 220°C/Gas 9.

6 Bake the bread in the preheated oven for about 10 minutes, then turn the temperature down to 170°C/Fan 150°C/Gas 3½ and bake for a further 15–20 minutes. Remove the sticks and place them on a rack to cool.

CHOCOLATE RYE BREAD

Although it contains cocoa powder, this bread is not sweet. The cocoa just gives it a great flavour and texture. I love this bread, as it is a bit different from the normal rye loaf and goes beautifully with savoury toppings such as Parma ham.

MAKES 1 LOAF

300g strong white flour, plus extra for dusting
125g rye flour
50g cocoa powder
9g fast-action dried yeast
1 tbsp vegetable oil
300ml water, room temperature
10g fine sea salt
30g golden caster sugar

1 Put the flours, cocoa powder and dried yeast in a bowl and mix them together with your hands. Add the oil and water and then start to bring the dough together with your hands. Add the salt and sugar and work them into the dough. Don't worry if the dough is very sticky and wet – the kneading process will bring it together.

2 Tip the dough on to a lightly floured work surface. Clean your hands and dust them with flour. Knead the dough by placing the 3 middle fingers of your left hand on the bottom part of the dough, then, using the palm of the other hand, push the dough away from you. Roll the dough back towards you and give it a half turn. Repeat the process for 10 minutes, remembering to give the dough a half turn each time.

3 Dust a clean bowl with flour, then roll the dough into a ball and put it in the bowl. Cover the bowl with cling film and leave the dough at room temperature to double in size.

4 Once the dough has doubled in size, put it on a lightly floured surface and knock it back by kneading it agan 3 times. Roll it into a ball, then place it on a floured baking tray and leave it to prove again until doubled in size. Preheat the oven to 220°C/Fan 200°C/Gas 7.

5 Place the bread in the preheated oven and bake for 10 minutes, then turn the temperature down to 180°C/Fan 160°C/Gas 4 and bake for a further 15 minutes. Remove the bread from the oven and place it on a wire rack to cool.

BROWN LOAF

This is an excellent brown bread and I like to make double the quantity and freeze a couple of loaves – it's really no more work. Allowing dough to rise naturally and slowly like this gives the best texture. Factory-made bread includes additives to speed up mixing and rising, so will never taste as good.

MAKES 2 LOAVES

700g strong white
  bread flour, plus
  extra for dusting
300g stoneground
  wholemeal flour
12g fast-action dried yeast
600ml water, room
  temperature
20g fine sea salt
vegetable oil, for greasing

1 Put the white and wholemeal flours in a bowl with the dried yeast and mix them together with your hands. Add the water and then, using one hand, start to bring the dough together.

2 Tip the dough on to a lightly floured work surface. Clean your hands and dust them with flour.

3 To knead the dough, place the 3 middle fingers of your left hand on the bottom part of the dough and, using the palm of the other hand, push the dough away from you. Roll the dough back towards you and give it a half turn. Repeat this process for 10 minutes, remembering to give the dough a half turn each time. Add the salt halfway through kneading and you will find the dough starts to become softer as the liquid comes out of the flour.

4 Dust a clean bowl with flour, then roll the dough into a ball and put it in the bowl. Cover the bowl with cling film and leave the dough at room temperature to double in size. Preheat the oven to 220°C/Fan 200°C/Gas 7.

5 Once the dough has doubled in size, tip it on to a floured work surface and knock it back by kneading it again 3 times. Do not tear the dough.

6 Oil a couple of 900g loaf tins. Cut the dough into 2 pieces and put them in the tins. Bake for 25 minutes, then turn the temperature down to 170°C/Fan 150°C/Gas 3½ and continue to bake for another 20 minutes. Remove the loaves from the oven and place them on a wire rack to cool.

RICH BREAD

Because of its richer content this bread has a longer shelf life than most. It also tastes divine, particularly when toasted and spread with salted butter and marmalade. So good. It freezes well too.

MAKES 1 LARGE OR 2 SMALL LOAVES

600g strong white
   bread flour, plus
   extra for dusting
10g fast-action dried yeast
80g butter
325ml whole milk
1 tsp golden caster sugar
1 egg, beaten
10g fine sea salt
1 egg yolk, mixed with
   1 tbsp water, to glaze
vegetable oil, for greasing

1 Mix the flour with the yeast in a large bowl. Gently melt the butter in a pan, then mix it with the milk, sugar and beaten egg. Stir this mixture into the flour and mix to a soft dough.

2 Tip the dough on to a lightly floured work surface and knead for 10 minutes. Add the salt and continue kneading and stretching for another 5 minutes. Put the dough into a clean, floured bowl, cover with cling film and allow it to rise until doubled in volume.

3 Oil a 900g loaf tin or 2 x 450g tins. Place the dough in the tin or tins, then leave to rise again until doubled in size. Brush the loaf or loaves with beaten egg yolk. Preheat the oven to 200°C/Fan 180°C/Gas 6.

4 Bake in the preheated oven for 30 minutes, Remove a loaf and tap the base – if it sounds hollow, it's done. Cool the bread on a wire rack.

PESTO BREAD

This is a tasty bread and it slices really well, so it's good for sandwiches.
Try it with chicken and salad or some mozzarella – delicious. You could
also make little pesto rolls by splitting the dough into 50-gram portions. I've
included a recipe for pesto here, but you could buy some if you prefer.

MAKES 2 LOAVES

500g strong white
    bread flour, plus
    extra for dusting
10g fast-action dried yeast
250ml water, room
    temperature
10g fine sea salt

Pesto
1 garlic clove, peeled
pinch of fine sea salt
15g pine nuts
125g basil, leaves picked
    from the stems
2 tbsp grated
    Parmesan cheese
125–150ml extra
    virgin olive oil
juice of ½ lemon

1 First make the pesto. Put the garlic and salt in a food processor and process, then add the pine nuts and crush them. Try not to overwork them. Add the basil leaves, a few at a time, and work them in as quickly as you can. Add the cheese and finally the oil and lemon juice to make a bright green paste. The quicker you bring the whole thing together, the less heat will be generated and the colour of the pesto will stay bright. The longer you work it, the darker it will look.

2 For the bread, place the flour and dried yeast into a bowl and mix them together with your hands. Add 75g of the pesto and the water to the flour, then using one hand start to bring the dough together. At this point, add the salt and work it into the dough. Don't worry if the dough is very sticky and wet – the kneading process will bring it together.

3 Tip the dough on to a lightly floured work surface. Clean your hands and dust them with flour. Knead the dough by placing the 3 middle fingers of your left hand on the bottom part of the dough, then, using the palm of the other hand, push the dough away from you. Roll the dough back towards you and give it a half turn. Repeat the process for 5 minutes, remembering to give the dough a half turn each time.

4 Dust a clean bowl with flour, put the dough in the bowl and cover it with cling film. Leave the dough at room temperature until doubled in size. Then tip the dough back on to a lightly floured surface and knock it back by kneading it again 3 times. Roll it into a ball and cut the dough into 2 even portions. Lightly flour 2 x 900g loaf tins.

5 Roll the dough into oval shapes roughly the same length as the tins, then place them in the tins. Leave them to double in size. Preheat the oven to 220°C/Fan 200°C/Gas 7.

6 Put the tins in the preheated oven and bake the loaves for 10 minutes, then turn the temperature down to 180°C/Fan 160°C/Gas 4 and bake for a further 15–20 minutes. Remove the loaves from the tins and place them on a wire rack to cool.

FOCACCIA

Home-made focaccia is a real treat. Brushing the bread with oil and adding a thin layer of oil to the baking tin gives it a lovely crunchy crust, which I adore. Delicious with cheese, salad or just dipped in some good olive oil.

MAKES 1 LOAF

450g strong white
   bread flour, plus
   extra for dusting
9g fast-action dried yeast
2 tsp fine sea salt
250ml water, room
   temperature
up to 100ml olive oil

Toppings
crushed garlic, rosemary
   leaves, flaked sea salt
sliced red onions, dried
   mint, coriander
   or cumin seeds,
   flaked sea salt

1 Place the flour in a large bowl. Make a well in the middle and add the yeast, salt, water and 25ml of the olive oil. Mix all the ingredients together with your hands to form a dough.

2 Tip the dough on to a lightly floured work surface. Clean your hands and dust them with flour. Knead the dough by placing the 3 middle fingers of your left hand on the bottom part of the dough, then, using the palm of the other hand, push the dough away from you. Roll the dough back towards you and give it a half turn. Repeat the process for 10 minutes, remembering to give the dough a half turn each time.

3 Put the kneaded dough into a large clean bowl and brush it with olive oil. Cover it loosely with cling film and leave to rise until it has doubled in size. After the dough has risen, knock it back by kneading again.

4 Pour a thin layer of oil into a rectangular baking tin, measuring roughly 22 x 32cm, then stretch the dough to fit into the tin. Pour enough olive oil over the dough to cover it lightly and, using your fingertips, press dents all over the top. Add whatever topping you are using, pressing it into the dough to help the flavours to penetrate. Then sprinkle a little more oil over the surface and some flaked sea salt. Leave the bread to rise again until doubled in size. Preheat the oven to 240°C/Fan 220°C/Gas 9.

5 Bake the bread in the preheated oven for 10 minutes, then turn the temperature down to 200°C/Fan 180°C/Gas 6 and bake for another 20 minutes. Remove the bread from the tin and place it on a wire rack to cool.

FIG AND GOATS' CHEESE BREAD

Once you've got the knack of breadmaking, try this recipe – it's an unusual bread and very delicious. I love goats' cheese anyway and the flavour goes so well with the figs. Serve a hunk of this with cheese, soup or just by itself.

MAKES 2 LOAVES

450g strong white
    bread flour, plus
    extra for dusting
11g fast-action dried yeast
2 tsp fine sea salt
25ml olive oil, plus
    extra for greasing
300ml water, room
    temperature

Toppings
5 dried figs
150g goats' cheese,
    crumbled

1 Place the flour in a large bowl, make a well in the middle and add the yeast, salt, oil and water. Mix all the ingredients together with your hands to form a dough. Tip the dough out on to a lightly floured work surface, then clean your hands and dust them with flour.

2 Start to knead the dough by placing the 3 middle fingers of your left hand on the bottom part of the dough and, using the palm of the other hand, push the dough away from you. Roll the dough back towards you and give it a half turn. Repeat this process for 10 minutes, remembering to give the dough a half turn each time.

3 Place the dough in a clean, lightly floured bowl, cover it loosely with cling film and leave it to rise until it has doubled in size.

4 Rehydrate the figs by placing them in a bowl of just-boiled water for 15 minutes. Drain them, then dice them finely and set them aside.

5 Once the dough has risen, knock it back by kneading it again 3 times. Oil a round 23cm cake tin, then roll out the dough into a circle to fit the tin. Add the goats' cheese and figs, pressing them into the dough to help the flavours penetrate. Leave the dough to rise again until it has doubled in size. Preheat the oven to 240°C/ Fan 220°C/Gas 9.

6 Bake the bread in the preheated oven for 10 minutes, then turn the oven down to 200°C/Fan 180°C/Gas 6 and bake for another 20 minutes. Remove the bread from the tin and place it on a wire rack to cool.

STOCKS & SAUCES

The chapter begins with basic stocks, then progresses, skill by skill, up to some showpiece sauces and a punchy piccalilli.

VEGETABLE STOCK

This is a simple stock, ideal for soups and vegetable risottos. I haven't given a quantity for this and the other stocks, as it depends on how much water you use to cover the ingredients.

1 onion, peeled and sliced
1 garlic bulb, cut in half crosswise
2 carrots, peeled and sliced
2 celery sticks, sliced
1 leek, white part only,
roughly chopped
handful of parsley stalks
4 black peppercorns

1 Put all the vegetables, parsley and peppercorns in a large pan. Add water to cover, then place the pan over a high heat and bring to the boil. Once the water is boiling, turn the heat down to medium and simmer gently for 20 minutes.

2 Turn off the heat and set the stock aside for 20 minutes. Pass the stock through a fine sieve and store in the fridge for 4 days or freeze until required.

VEGETABLE NAGE

A nage is stronger and more flavoursome than a stock and is used as a poaching liquid for chicken and fish. You can also reduce it and use it to make a sauce.

6 carrots, peeled and chopped
1 white onion, peeled
and chopped
1 garlic bulb, cut in
half crosswise

1 head of celery, roughly chopped
½ celeriac, peeled and chopped
1 leek, white part only,
roughly chopped
750ml white wine
zest and juice of 2 lemons
20 coriander seeds
2 star anise
2 juniper berries
2 cardamom seeds
1 tbsp fennel seeds
20 white peppercorns
15 pink peppercorns
bunches of chervil,
tarragon and parsley

1 Put all the vegetables in a large stock pot. Add cold water to cover, then place the pan over a high heat and bring to the boil. Once boiling, turn the heat down to medium and simmer for 30 minutes. Add the white wine, lemon zest and juice and all the spices, turn up the heat and bring back to the boil. Reduce the heat again and simmer for 5 minutes, then remove and set aside to infuse and cool.

2 Strain the liquid into a bowl, add all the herbs and place the nage in the fridge for 24 hours so the flavours can infuse.

3 Strain again, discard the herbs and store in the fridge. Use within 3 days or freeze and use when required.

WHITE CHICKEN STOCK

A light stock with no colour, this is good for fish dishes as well as chicken and for white sauces. Ask your butcher for raw chicken carcasses.

1 large white onion, peeled
and roughly chopped
1 leek, white part only,
roughly chopped
1 garlic bulb, cut in
half crosswise
1 head of celery, roughly chopped
10 parsley sprigs
10 thyme sprigs
2 bay leaves
8 black peppercorns
350ml white wine
2 raw chicken carcasses

1 Put the onion, leek, garlic and
celery in a large stock pot with the
herbs and peppercorns. Pour in the
white wine, then place the pot over
a high heat until the wine is reduced
by half.

2 Break up the chicken carcasses,
add them to the pan and then cover
with cold water and bring to the boil.
Turn the heat down to medium, skim
off any scum with a ladle, then leave
to simmer for 1 hour. Keep skimming
as necessary.

3 Remove the pan from the heat and
leave the stock to infuse and cool
slightly. Skim one more time, then
remove the bones and vegetables
and discard them. Strain the stock
through a fine sieve or cloth. Store
the stock in the fridge and use within
3 days or freeze and use when
needed.

BROWN CHICKEN STOCK

*This has a nuttier, richer flavour
than white chicken stock and
is good for meat dishes.*

2 chicken carcasses
(raw or cooked)
1 tsp vegetable oil
1 large white onion, peeled
and roughly chopped
2 carrots, peeled and
roughly chopped
1 celery stick, roughly chopped
1 leek, white part only,
roughly chopped
1 garlic bulb, cut in
half crosswise
100g tomato purée
1 litre red wine
bunch of parsley
6 thyme sprigs
3 bay leaves
8 black peppercorns

1 Preheat the oven to 200°C/Fan 180°C/
Gas 6. Put the chicken carcasses in
a deep roasting tin and roast them
in the oven for about 40 minutes,
or until nicely browned.

2 Heat the oil in a very large pan over
a medium-high heat. Add all the
vegetables and cook until browned,
then add the tomato purée and cook
for 2 minutes. Transfer the chicken
bones to the pan and remove most
of the fat from the roasting tin.
Pour the red wine into the tin and
boil until reduced by about a third,
scraping up any sticky bits from the
bottom of the tin, then add this to
the pan.

3 Add enough cold water to the pan to
cover the bones, then add the herbs
and peppercorns. Bring to the boil,
then turn the heat down and skim
any scum from the surface. Simmer
for 1½ hours, skimming when
necessary.

4 Take the pan off the heat and set the stock aside to cool slightly. Remove the bones and strain the stock through a fine sieve or cloth. Place in the fridge and use within 3 days or freeze.

FISH STOCK

It's not hard to make a good fish stock and it is so much better than bought. It will really make a difference to your dish. Fishmongers are always happy to give you fish bones.

2kg turbot or plaice bones
(or any white fish), gills
and eyes removed
1 onion, peeled and
roughly chopped
1 leek, white part only,
roughly chopped
1 fennel bulb, roughly chopped
1 garlic bulb, cut in
half crosswise
200ml white wine (optional)
5 black peppercorns
1 bay leaf
handful of parsley stalks
juice of 1 lemon

1 Rinse the fish bones well under cold running water. Put them in a large pan, cover with cold water and bring to the boil. Once the water is boiling, turn the heat down to a simmer and use a ladle to skim off all the scum that has risen to the top. This will stop the stock being cloudy.

2 Add the vegetables and wine, if using, and bring back to the boil – if you don't want to use wine, add

an extra 200ml of water. Then turn the heat down and simmer for 20 minutes, skimming any scum that appears. Add the peppercorns, bay leaf, parsley stalks and the lemon juice. Take the pan off the heat, set it aside for 15 minutes, then pass it through a fine sieve lined with muslin. Keep the stock in the fridge and use within 3 days or freeze it and use when required.

DUCK OR GAME STOCK

Both these are delicious, richly flavoured stocks to use with duck or game dishes.

4 raw duck carcasses, broken
up, or 2kg venison bones
1 tsp vegetable oil
1 onion, peeled and
roughly chopped
1 carrot, peeled and
roughly chopped
1 celery stick,
roughly chopped
1 leek, white part only,
roughly chopped
1 garlic bulb, cut in
half crosswise
75g tomato purée
1 litre red wine
bunch of parsley
10 thyme sprigs
4 bay leaves
8 black peppercorns

1 Preheat the oven to 200°C/Fan 180°C/ Gas 6. Place the duck or venison bones in a deep roasting tin and roast for about 40 minutes or until nicely browned.

2 Heat the oil in a large pan over a medium-high heat. Add the vegetables and cook until browned, then add the tomato purée and cook for another 2 minutes. Transfer the duck or venison bones to the pan, then tip out most of the fat from the roasting tin. Add the red wine to the tin and stir over the heat until reduced by about a third, scraping up any sticky bits from the bottom of the tin, then add to the pan.

3 Cover the bones with cold water and add the herbs and peppercorns. Bring to the boil, then turn the heat down and skim off any scum from the surface. Simmer for 2 hours, skimming when necessary. You may need to add more water if the level gets too low.

4 Take the pan off the heat and set aside for the stock to cool slightly. Remove the bones and strain the stock through a fine sieve or cloth. Place the stock in the fridge and use within 3 days or freeze it.

LAMB STOCK

This stock does take a while to cook but it's well worth it. It adds lots of flavour to your dish.

3kg lamb bones
1 tbsp vegetable oil
2 carrots, peeled and sliced
1 white onion, peeled
and quartered
2 celery sticks, roughly chopped
1 garlic bulb, cut in
half crosswise
50g tomato purée

450ml red wine
4 rosemary or thyme sprigs
3 bay leaves
large bunch of parsley
8 black peppercorns

1 Preheat the oven to 200°C/Fan 180°C/Gas 6. Put the bones in a large roasting tin and roast them for about 40 minutes until nicely browned.

2 Heat the oil in a large pan over a medium heat. Add the carrots, onion, celery and garlic and cook until browned. Add the tomato purée and cook for another minute.

3 Remove the bones from the roasting tin and place them in the pan. Remove most of the fat from the roasting tin, then pour in the red wine and place over a medium heat. Deglaze the tin, scraping up any sticky bits from the base, then continue to cook to reduce the liquid. Add this to the pan with the herbs and peppercorns, then add cold water to cover the bones.

4 Bring the stock to the boil over a high heat, then skim off any scum that has formed. Turn the heat down to medium and simmer very gently for 2 hours, skimming when necessary.

5 Take the pan off the heat and set it aside for the stock to cool slightly. Remove the bones and strain the stock through a sieve into a large bowl. Place in the fridge and chill overnight, then skim any fat off the surface. Use within 3 days or freeze and use as required.

STOCKS & SAUCES

BEEF STOCK

This is a lovely rich beef stock and the longer you can cook it the better it is. It does take a bit of time but it is worth it.

4kg beef bones
1 tbsp vegetable oil
2 carrots, peeled and
roughly chopped
2 onions, peeled and quartered
2 sticks celery, roughly chopped
1 leek, white part only,
roughly chopped
1 garlic bulb, cut in
half crosswise
100g tomato purée
1 litre red wine
8 black peppercorns
2 bay leaves
8 parsley stalks
6 thyme sprigs

1 Preheat the oven to 200°C/Fan 180°C/ Gas 6. Put the bones in a roasting tin and roast for about 40 minutes until well browned.

2 Heat the oil in the largest pan you've got over a medium heat, then add the carrots, onions, celery, leek and garlic and cook until browned. Add the tomato purée and cook for 1 minute.

3 Remove the bones from the roasting tin and add them to the pan. Pour off most of the fat from the tin, then add the red wine. Place the tin over a medium heat and stir, scraping up any sticky bits, and boil the wine for a couple of minutes. Add it to the pan with the peppercorns, bay leaves, parsley stalks and thyme, then fill the pan with enough cold water to cover the bones.

4 Bring the stock to the boil over a high heat and skim off any scum that forms. Turn the heat down and leave the stock to simmer very gently for 3–4 hours. From time to time, skim off any scum.

5 Take the pan off the heat and set it aside to allow the stock to cool slightly. Then remove the bones and strain the stock through a sieve into a large bowl. Place the stock in the fridge and chill overnight, then skim off any fat from the surface. Use within 3 days or freeze and use as needed.

LIGHT TOMATO SAUCE

Make this in the summer when tomatoes are at their best – and cheapest. It's ideal if you grow your own and you have a glut. If you do want to make this sauce with canned tomatoes, use the whole ones and drain them.

MAKES 1 LITRE
1kg really ripe fresh tomatoes
2 tbsp olive oil
150g finely chopped onion
1 garlic clove, peeled
and finely chopped
1 tsp dried thyme
1 tsp caster sugar
1 tsp tomato purée
20 basil leaves
fine sea salt and black pepper

1 First skin the tomatoes. Plunge them into a pan of boiling water and count to 30 seconds, then remove them with a slotted spoon and put them in a bowl of cold water. The skins should peel off easily. Chop the tomatoes, keeping all the juice.

2 Heat the olive oil in a large pan, add the onion and let it soften for about 5 minutes. Add the garlic, thyme, chopped tomatoes and their juice. Bring to a simmer and cook for about 25 minutes over a low heat. Halfway through this time, add the sugar, tomato purée and half the basil, then put a lid on the pan so the sauce doesn't reduce too much. Season to taste and add the rest of the basil.

RICH TOMATO SAUCE

The longer you cook this, the thicker and richer it becomes. It's nice on pizza and also goes beautifully with oily fish. If you do use canned tomatoes, choose the whole ones rather than the chopped. They taste better.

MAKES 1 LITRE
4 tbsp extra virgin olive oil
1 large white onion, peeled
and finely chopped
1 red pepper, seeded
and finely chopped
2 tbsp balsamic vinegar
2 garlic cloves, peeled
and finely chopped
1 dessert spoon of chopped
fresh oregano or 1 tsp dried
1kg fresh tomatoes or
3 cans of tomatoes, drained
200ml vegetable stock
(if using fresh tomatoes)
3 bay leaves
15 basil leaves
2 tbsp tomato purée
fine sea salt and black pepper

1 Heat the oil in a large pan, then add the onion and red pepper and cook until softened. Add the balsamic vinegar, garlic and oregano and cook for a further minute.

2 If using fresh tomatoes, put them in a pan of boiling water and simmer for 30 seconds. Remove them with a slotted spoon and plunge them into a bowl of cold water, then peel off the skins. Chop roughly and add them to the onion and pepper mix, then add the stock, if using fresh tomatoes. For canned tomatoes, just add the drained tomatoes to the pan.

3 Add the bay leaves and basil, mix well and continue cooking over a low heat for a further 20 minutes, uncovered. Tip everything into a food processor, add the tomato purée and blitz. Season well.

4 Put the mixture back into the pan and cook for a further 15 minutes to make a thick, flavoursome sauce. Season again if needed. If you want to keep the sauce for a few days, put it in a bowl and add a layer of olive oil. Store the sauce in the fridge.

APPLE SAUCE

I love apple sauce with pork but it also goes well with chicken and barbecued food. I like to use Cox apples as well as Bramleys for sweetness.

MAKES A GOOD BOWLFUL
500g Bramley apples (about 2 medium)
200g Cox apples (about 2 medium)
juice of 1 lemon
1 cinnamon stick
50g golden caster sugar
15g butter
fine sea salt

1 Peel and core the apples and slice them finely. Put the apples in a pan with the lemon juice and cinnamon stick and mix well. Place the pan over a low heat and gently cook the apple until soft.

2 Add the sugar and cook the sauce for a further minute until it thickens. I like to mash the apple rather than process it because I like some texture in my sauce. Finish with the butter and a little salt to taste.

MADEIRA CREAM SAUCE

A rich but simple sauce, this goes well with steak, venison and other game. If you like, you could add some sautéed wild mushrooms.

MAKES 350–400ML
500g chicken bones,
chopped up small
150ml Madeira
150ml double cream
150ml white chicken stock
juice of ½ lemon
fine sea salt and white pepper

1 Preheat the oven to 180°C/Fan 160°C/ Gas 4. Place the chicken bones in a roasting tin and roast for about 45 minutes until golden brown.

2 Remove the bones from the tin and put them in a large pan with the Madeira, cream and stock. Place over a medium-high heat and bring to the boil, then simmer until the sauce is reduced to about 250ml.

3 Take the pan off the heat and pass the sauce through a fine sieve.

Season to taste with salt, pepper and lemon juice.

TAPENADE

I love having a bowl of this to enjoy as a snack with sticks of raw vegetables or crackers. It's also really good spread on grilled fish.

SERVES 4
400g black olives, pitted
100g anchovies, drained and chopped
40g small capers
juice of 1 lemon
1 red chilli, seeded
1 garlic clove, peeled and
finely chopped
80ml olive oil
small bunch of flatleaf
parsley, roughly chopped

1 Put the olives, anchovies, capers, lemon juice, chilli and garlic into a food processor. Process for about 20 seconds – you want a roughly chopped mixture, not a purée.

2 Tip the mixture into a bowl and stir in the olive oil and parsley. Use right away or store in an airtight container in the fridge. If you want to keep it for a few days, add a layer of olive oil on the top.

RED PEPPER SAUCE

This is an excellent flavoursome sauce that's great with so many things, such as sea bass, cod, chicken or pasta.

SERVES 4
3 red peppers

150ml olive oil
2 banana shallots, peeled
and finely diced
2 garlic cloves, unpeeled
20ml balsamic vinegar
50ml vegetable stock (if needed)
fine sea salt

1 Preheat the oven to 180°C/Fan 160°C/Gas 4. Cut the peppers in half lengthways and remove the seeds and white pith. Gently heat 50ml of the oil in an ovenproof pan, then add the diced shallots. Let them soften without colouring, then add the red peppers and garlic. Cover the pan with foil and bake in the oven for 40 minutes.

2 Remove the pan from the oven and add the balsamic vinegar. Tip the contents of the pan into a food processor and blend to a fine purée. Stir in the rest of the olive oil and then strain the purée through a fine sieve. The sauce should be thick enough to coat the back of a spoon, but if it's too thick, thin it down with the vegetable stock. This sauce keeps well in the fridge for up to 3 days.

CHUNKY SAUCE VIERGE

A rustic version of sauce vierge (see page 134), this is easy to prepare and good with fish and meat, particularly barbecued dishes. Keeps well in the fridge for a couple of days.

SERVES 4
1 banana shallot, peeled
and finely diced
1 small garlic clove, peeled

and very finely chopped
8 cherry tomatoes, quartered
25g small capers, drained
150ml olive oil
15g sherry vinegar
5g each of tarragon, chervil
and parsley, finely chopped
fine sea salt and black pepper

1 Put all the ingredients in a bowl, mix well and season with salt and pepper. Store in the fridge until needed.

MUSHROOM SAUCE

Quick and simple to make, this is great with chicken and works as an accompaniment as well as a sauce.

SERVES 4
50g butter
30ml vegetable oil
1 banana shallot, peeled
and finely diced
1 garlic clove, peeled
and finely diced
3 thyme sprigs, leaves only
250g button mushrooms,
wiped and sliced
150ml double cream
50ml vegetable stock
juice of 1 lemon
fine sea salt

1 Heat the butter and oil in a large pan over a medium heat. Add the shallot, garlic and thyme leaves and cook for 5 minutes or until the shallots start to brown. Add the mushrooms and cook until soft.

2 Pour in the double cream and vegetable stock, then bring to the boil

and simmer for 5 minutes. Blend the sauce to a smooth purée in a food processor, then season with lemon juice and salt to taste. If the sauce seems lumpy, pass it through a fine sieve.

BREAD SAUCE

For me, turkey or chicken with a good bread sauce is a marriage made in heaven. This is a creamy version.

SERVES 6–8
600g white bread
1 litre whole milk
8 cloves
2 bay leaves
6 black peppercorns
30g butter
100ml double cream
fine sea salt

1 Remove the crusts from the bread and discard them. Put the bread in a blender or food processor and blitz to crumbs.

2 Pour the milk into a pan and add the cloves, bay leaves, peppercorns and a teaspoon of salt. Bring to the boil and then set aside for at least 20 minutes for the ingredients to infuse. Pass the milk through a fine sieve and then pour it back into the pan. Warm the milk over a medium heat, then add the breadcrumbs and cook for about 10 minutes, stirring every so often.

3 Add the butter and double cream and stir until the butter has melted and combined with the sauce. Check the seasoning and add more salt if necessary.

BEURRE BLANC

A delicious buttery sauce, this goes well with vegetables and white meat but is particularly heavenly with fish. You can add extra flavourings, such as fresh tarragon, vermouth, lemon or even ginger syrup, after whisking in the butter.

MAKES 200ML
1 banana shallot, peeled and finely chopped
60ml white wine vinegar
60ml white wine
110g cold butter, diced small
10 chives, finely snipped
fine sea salt (optional)

1 Place the chopped shallot in a pan with the vinegar and white wine, then bring to a simmer over a medium heat. Cook for 2 minutes, or until the liquid has reduced to about 30ml.

2 Lower the heat and gradually whisk in the butter, a little at a time, until the mixture is well combined and thickened. Strain the sauce into a bowl, stir in the chives and season with salt if needed. Best used right away.

BÉCHAMEL SAUCE

This basic but tasty white sauce is good with fish, chicken – practically anything. You can add extra flavourings such as grated cheese.

MAKES 450ML
450ml whole milk
1 bay leaf

50g sliced onion
2 thyme sprigs (optional)
5 black peppercorns
40g butter
40g plain flour
fine sea salt

1 Pour the milk into a pan and add the bay leaf, onion, thyme, if using, and peppercorns. Heat the milk to simmering point, then set it aside to infuse. It's good to do this the night before you make the sauce, if possible.

2 Melt the butter in a pan, add the flour and stir to make a paste – this is called a 'roux'. Gradually add the milk, stirring all the time to prevent lumps forming. Season with salt.

3 If the sauce is at all lumpy, strain it through a fine sieve into a bowl – it should be silky and smooth. It is now ready to use.

PICCALILLI

I love to have a couple of jars of this tasty vegetable pickle in my fridge. It's great served with cheese and cold meats. You can buy it, but home-made is so much better.

MAKES 2 BIG JARS
1 cucumber, peeled,
seeded and diced
50g green beans,
topped and tailed
1 cauliflower, split into
really small florets
8 shallots, peeled and finely diced
500ml white wine vinegar
250ml malt vinegar

300g caster sugar
55g English mustard powder
14g ground turmeric
3 tbsp cornflour

1 Sprinkle the diced cucumber with salt, put it in a sieve and leave it to drain for 20 minutes. Cut the green beans into small pieces about the same size as the cucumber. Rinse the salt from the cucumber and pat it all dry. Put it in a large bowl with the rest of the vegetables.

2 Pour the vinegars into a pan and bring them to the boil over a high heat. Boil for 1 minute, then remove the pan from the heat.

3 Mix the sugar, mustard, turmeric and cornflour in a bowl with 50ml of the boiled vinegar to make a paste. Place the pan with the vinegar over a high heat and bring back to the boil. Stir in the paste and boil until thick enough to coat the back of a spoon.

4 Pour the hot liquid over the vegetables, then spoon the mixture into sterilised Kilner jars (see page 103). Allow to cool, store in the fridge and use as needed.

STOCKS &
SAUCES

INDEX

INDEX

ACKNOWLEDGEMENTS

This book has meant a great deal to me and I have so enjoyed writing it, but it would not exist without the team. I would like to thank Lizzy Gray, the publishing director who commissioned the book, for believing in me. I would also like to thank Charlotte Macdonald, my first book editor, who was with me at the outset, then went on maternity leave to have her lovely little girl. Isabel Hayman-Brown stepped into some very large shoes and did an amazing job; she was always very calm and very encouraging. Then there is the wonderful Jinny, who had such patience and dedication and understanding, and was always suggesting I go back and write more! I think she is a marvel.

A big thank you to my chefs Iain More and Lee Wood for all their input and for helping me set out the book as a cookery course. Also, thank you to Liz Wendt for the hours she spent testing recipes, sometimes at very short notice.

Thank you to the most amazing photo-shoot team: Lisa Harrison and her assistant Evie Harbury for the wonderful cooking, Andrew Hayes Watkins for the fabulous photos, prop stylist Olivia Wardle, and hair and make up artist Nicky Clarke. What a team! Thanks, too, to Gemma Wilson and Two Associates for the beautiful design.

Thank you to everyone at Hadlow College for their support – Nadia Needham, for producing the drawings of the meat and poultry cuts, Neil Lakeland, head of marketing, and especially to Mark Lumston-Taylor, who always encourages me in everything I do. Thank you also to Iain Fleming for the incredible herb wall.

I'd also like to thank the publicity and marketing people at Ebury – Claire Scott, Lottie Huckle and all the other people at Ebury who have helped me.

To my book agent, Heather Holden-Brown – thank you for all your help and support. And thanks to Anne Kibel, my television agent, who works with the marketing team on publicity for the book.

Last but not least, Martin Sweeney, who organises and coordinates my life at the cookery school; without him I would be lost.